CU00660288

Discovering Island Writers
Exploring the Literary Tradition of the Isle of Wight

First Published in Great Britain in 2001 by Island Books
Copyright 2001 by Brian Hinton
Photographs Copyright 2001 by Neil Hammerton & Duncan Knifton
The moral right of the author has been asserted
A CIP catalogue record for this book is available from the British Library
ISBN 1 898198 09 8

Design by Percy Westwood, production by Prontaprint, Isle of Wight,
Unit 4, Manners View, Dodnor, Newport, isle of Wight PO30 5FA

ISLAND BOOKS

i

Also by Brian Hinton

Bitter End, a Story (Oxford, privately printed) 1972

Poems From An Island (IOW Poetry Society) 1981, with Val Berry

The Old Changing Way (IOW Poetry Society) 1982

Sotonians (IOW Poetry Society) 1984, with Deryk Soord

*The Farringford Journal of Emily Tennyson 1853-1864 edited
with Richard J Hutchings (IOW County Press) 1986*

Breasting the Tide (KQBX Press) 1986

The Heart's Clockwork (Enitharmon) 1989 with illustrations by Julian Bell

Nights in Wight Satin (IOW Council) 1990

*Immortal Faces, Julia Margaret Cameron on the Isle of Wight
(IOW County Press & IOW Council) 1992*

Whodunit, a poem (Ure Group Press) 1994

*Wight, An Island From The Air (Island Books) 1994 with
photographs by Brian Manby*

*Wight, An Island From The Air: The Second Flight (Island Books) 1995
with photographs by Brian Manby*

*Message To Love, The Isle of Wight Festivals 1968-1970
(Castle Communications) 1995*

Ties (Tears in the Fence) 1995

'A Dorset Sequence' in Dorset Contours (East Street Poets) 1996

Joni Mitchell - Both Sides Now (Sanctuary) 1996

Celtic Crossroads, the Art of Van Morrison (Sanctuary) 1997

Let Them All Talk, the Music of Elvis Costello (Sanctuary) 1999

Country Road, How Country Came to Nashville (Sanctuary) 2000

Contents

Dedication

Discovering Island Writers is the first step towards compiling a literary map of the Isle of Wight. Such an enterprise is by its very nature a collective one and although I have sampled all kinds of literary composition – with the occasional foray into the visual and musical arts – I have restricted comment to what can loosely be described as 'professional' writing. This is not to decry the vast body of self-produced or 'amateur' work in print, especially poetry, but I would need considerably more time than I have available to collect it, and much more space to include it.

I would recommend *any* writing about the Island and if I have not mentioned a particular author, it is probably through my own ignorance, rather than as a value judgement. After all, my own first publication on an Island theme, *Poems From An Island* (1981) was only made possible through a grant from the Isle of Wight Council for the Arts and I am forever grateful to them for giving me my chance.

I would like to dedicate this book to the memory of Richard Hutchings from whom I learnt so much and Neil Hammerton who encouraged me to undertake it in the first place.

Brian Hinton

Publisher's Note

Discovering Island Writers is not a guidebook in the accepted sense of the word although it can be used as one with Yarmouth as the starting and finishing point, or indeed any one of the many other towns and villages listed on a roughly circular route that embraces the whole island.

Brian Hinton's odyssey of literary achievement and endeavour entertains and informs as he journeys from Alfred Tennyson to Phillip Norman, Algernon Swinburne to Margaret Campbell Barnes, Robert Graves to David Gascoyne, and many other writers, familiar and unfamiliar, on whom the island has exercised a powerful influence.

Since the untimely death of Richard Hutchings in 1991, the literary history of the Isle of Wight has been sadly neglected. Brian Hinton's book, the first in a proposed trilogy, corrects this in a way that will encourage the reader to continue exploring the many rich and varied treasures he reveals.

I offer no apology for persuading Brian Hinton to include some of his own poetry in this book. A recent collection, *The Heart's Clockwork*, was published to extensive critical acclaim. "It should be evident that Hinton is an important poet . . . with the craftsmanship and sensibility of a real poet" wrote one reviewer.

All the photographs have been specially taken for this book. Many are of private houses and I am deeply grateful for the ready permission that has been given for their use.

Inevitably, between the writing of this book and its publication, changes have occurred — the ambitious plans for Golden Hill Fort appear to have been postponed; Glenbrook St Francis—once the dower house of Lady May Tennyson—has been demolished; Arreton Manor and the Peacock Vane are now in private hands; Kevin Mitchell has published *Newport Pubs* and Gay Baldwin's new book *Ghost Island* proved once and for all that this is the most haunted county in Britain. These and other amendments will be included in the next edition of *Discovering Island Writers* — feel free to write!

The current edition of *Perry's Guide Maps to the Isle of Wight* has been invaluable and any reader wishing to visit the locations referred to in **Discovering Island Writers**, will find it immensely useful.

Neil Hammerton

List of Illustrations

Front cover: The Old Mill, Yarmouth

Introduction

A Summer Isle of Eden lying in a purple belt of sea.

Tennyson

The Isle of Wight has long attracted writers to its wild shorelines and quiet lanes, its magical tumble of chalk downs, seascapes and secret habitations. As Alfred, Lord Tennyson wrote shortly after moving to the Island in 1853,

> *Half-lost in the liquid azure bloom of a crescent of sea, The silent-sapphire spangled marriage ring of the land*

Maud: A Monodrama (1855)

Conflict and resolution are the two opposing elements of Island scenery. For some Wight is a retreat from the everyday world, a fantasy Island where everything is possible. If, as is likely, the young William Shakespeare visited with a group of strolling players, The Tempest captures much of this strangeness. It ends with Prospero, and by implication the author, breaking his magical staff and leaving for home, a mere man. Some visiting writers, Charles Darwin, John Keats, J B Priestley, have found their initial delight turn to repulsion, like a love affair gone sour. It is outsiders who have usually stayed, and locals who have emigrated as soon as they possibly could, while later expressing a deep nostalgia for the lost Eden of childhood. Many have recorded the profound impact a short stay on the Island has had upon them, a touchstone of something approaching paradise.

In **Discovering Island Writers** I have tried to include a taste of all those connected with the Isle of Wight who have made their living with words, from Hollywood scriptwriters to authors of sermons, from poets to scientists. Anyone, indeed, who has converted 'Wight' to 'write', and found fresh words with which to somehow capture its unique spirit. We will circle the Island's rough diamond, starting and ending at Yarmouth, taking excursions inland as we go. Most of the places mentioned can still be seen. On this literary map modern day pilgrims can retrace ancient journeys seen through long dead eyes

> *We walk taller in their footsteps, fading on the sand.*

Brian Hinton: from Literary Haunts (1989)

and discover a vast variety of riches which the small compass of Wight magically contains. The same places are seen through the eyes of radically different writers, providing secret histories and bizarre parallels. 'Only connect' wrote E M Forster, prior to his visit here between the two World Wars.

As with the Island's strange geology, different time zones compact and twist to the surface to reveal unexpected confluences. Through a never accidental geography, Bob

1

Dylan meets Alfred, Lord Tennyson, John Osborne encounters Alfred Noyes, and Henry Fielding becomes a precursor to 'Some Mothers Do 'Ave 'Em'. Previous accounts of Island writers, in particular the pioneering work of Richard Hutchings, have concentrated on the great Romantic poets and the high Victorians. I hope here to widen the focus, to see how writers have been drawn here by social and artistic forces of which they were themselves unaware.

With the benefit of history, we will trace how writers were first attracted across the Solent to the great manor houses and their aristocratic patrons, for an upmarket version of the country weekend. During the chaos of the English Civil War, for some the Island acted not as a refuge but as a prison. In the 18th century, Wight became an English adjunct to the Continent, a place of grandeur and wild scenery.

Conversely, the Undercliff, the Island's own Deep South, came to provide, for the early 19th century, a calm almost magical presence, a healing ground. Here many poets found temporary solace, some emotionally, some physically through its warm sea breezes, a balm to weak chests. With Queen Victoria and Alfred, Lord Tennyson both in residence, the Island became the hub of Empire.

Later, with the new enthusiasm for beaches and bathing, many authors gained early memories of sun and sea, brought by their parents to the 'Holiday Isle'. Now the wheel has turned full circle, and those modern patrons of the Arts, the Arts Council and the National Lottery, have again drawn professional writers here, not for polite entertainment but for pay.

We will also discover how the Island gave refuge to those who wished to form an artistic community far from the madding crowd. **Bonchurch, Farringford, Osborne,** all drew their share of acolytes and old friends. Writers are still attracted here by ideas which combine the social and the spiritual. Gurdjieff's ritual dances, the pop music festivals of the late sixties, Christian retreats, ecological and occult awareness: all have left their imprint in words. This is the importance of any proper tradition. That it continues.

After all, the poets were here; – Keats, Swinburne, Tennyson . . . all writing hard, but beautifully. And is it too fanciful to suggest that some of this magic could be traced to them? Would it have been the same place if it had been the favourite resort of loan sharks, asset strippers, property developers? I think not. A different mental-spiritual atmosphere would have been created, and it would have lingered on.

J B Priestley

We are safely landed: let our journey begin . . .

Brian Hinton
Totland Bay
June 2000

Chapter One
Yarmouth, Totland & Freshwater Bay

Viewed from the Lymington ferry, the West Wight stretches across the horizon like a green snake ensnaring its willing prey, its highest summit surmounted by Tennyson's granite cross. We disembark under the forbidding walls of Henry VIII's castle designed to repel all invaders. A library of short stories could be written about the greetings and partings enacted here. In earlier times, paddle-steamers would berth at the end of the pier. In 1853, Tennyson and his wife missed the last one of the day, and made the crossing in a rowing boat. As Emily later wrote in her Journal, *It was a still November evening. One dark heron flew over the Solent backed by a daffodil sky.*

It was here in 1926 that Christopher Isherwood recorded the arrival of his friend W H Auden, striding down its timbers,

> *. . . a tall figure with loose violent impatient movements, dressed in dirty grey flannels and a black evening bow-tie. On his straw-coloured head was planted a very broad-brimmed black felt hat.*
>
> Christopher Isherwood: Lions and Shadows: An Education in the Twenties (1938)

It was here too that the diarist William Allingham met pioneer photographer Julia Margaret Cameron, another eccentrically dressed genius.

> *Saturday December 26th 1863. At Yarmouth I find Mrs Cameron shopping, who gives me a seat in her carriage, and tells me she has a copy of Henry Taylor's Works as a Christmas box. In a subsequent examination, which she put me through as to my opinion of HT's poetry, I fear my answering fell decidedly below her expectation, for the Christmas box was never given, nor did either of us mention it afterwards.*
>
> William Allingham: A Diary 1824-1889 (1907)

Yarmouth has long been a centre for yachting. Local authors include Adlard Coles, who produced the definitive *Creeks and Harbours of the Solent,* and Lady Cicely Gould, who wrote a novel entitled *Living River,* and *Gossip,* the lively history of her yacht of the same name. C W R 'Ron' Winter landed here long enough to write a definitive history of the place, *The Ancient Town of Yarmouth* (1981). He has since written much more about the Island, recording its manor houses, churches and famous characters.

In 1954, the historian A J P Taylor bought the Old Mill, from where he planned CND rallies with his friend J B Priestley. Yarmouth also provides the setting for Jill Chaney's

Yarmouth Pier — It was here in 1928 that Christopher Isherwood recorded the arrival of his friend W H Auden, striding down its timbers . . . *a tall figure with loose violent impatient movements, dressed in grey flannels and a black evening bow tie.*

Yarmouth — The Old Mill – Historian A J P Taylor planned CND rallies with his friend J B Priestley from here in the 1950s.

4

novel for older children, *Vectis Diary* (1979), a charming account of two girls who take holiday jobs, which ends with a murderer unmasked.

The Island is a place where the ancient and demonic nestle up to the everyday. Children used to go from house to house in Yarmouth every New Year's Eve singing the wassail song. This dates from a time before language was even written down, when rhyme and rhythm were allied to magic.

Wassail, Wassail to our town,
The cup is white, the ale is brown;
The cup is made of ashen tree,
And so is the ale of good barley.

Little maid, little maid turn the pin,
Open the door and let me in;
Joy be there, and joy be here,
We wish you all a Happy New Year.

Traditional

Every Guy Fawke's night, the citizenry circle the town with burning torches and half-hidden behind billowing clouds of tarry smoke, progress to a Viking-like bonfire on the cold beach.

From Yarmouth, taxis and buses take off for all parts of the Island. We cannot promise everyday the conversation, or rather monologue, which Auden delivered on the bus ride, in 'resonant Oxonian tones', and which was probably a direct attack on Tennyson himself.

Of course, intellect's the only thing that matters at all . . . apart from
Nature, geometry's all there is . . . Man's got to assert himself against
Nature, all the time . . . Poetry's got to be made up of images of form. I
hate sunsets and flowers. And I loathe the sea. The sea is formless . . .
Christopher Isherwood: Lions and Shadows: An Education in the Twenties (1938)

We will take, in our imagination, the open-topped bus to Alum Bay (from the upper deck of which glimpses of that very sea can still stop the heart) across the drawbridge under which the Yar makes its exit to the sea, and into **Hallet's Shute.** Best-selling novelist Jeffrey Archer often visited the Savoy Country Club here in the 80s to address meetings of the Isle of Wight Conservative Association.

A A Milne, author of *Winnie the Pooh* came to **Golden Hill Fort** in 1915 with the Warwickshire Rifles, in training for his spell in the trenches during the Great War. He later wrote that, while at the Fort, *I never fired a shot in anger, and only twelve under the influence of any other emotion. They all missed the Musketry Instructor, but hit the Isle of Wight – it was he who was angry.*

The Fort, built on Lord Palmerston's orders between 1863 and 1867, is at the time of writing, being turned into a kind of psychedelic theme park, inspired by the imagination of, amongst others, Hollywood film producer Robert Watts. He was location manager for the early James Bond films, and in charge of production on Stanley Kubrick's *2001 A Space Odyssey.* He became associate producer of the *Star Wars Trilogy,* produced the later Indiana Jones movies, and *Who Framed Roger Rabbit,* a startling combination of real actors and animation. Watts also recently co-produced the cartoon *American Tail II –*

Fievel Goes West with his old friend Stephen Spielberg. With that kind of imagination unleashed upon the West Wight, one awaits the feature films that are surely bound to follow.

The ornate, octagonal fort is likely to double as a film set, while its pub and restaurant have been renamed after Jimi Hendrix bands 'The Experience', and 'The Band of Gypsies'. Both locations contain relevant memorabilia from the 1970 Isle of Wight Pop Festival, the last major performance by Hendrix.

Golden Hill Fort reopened to the public after extensive alterations and refurbishment on midsummer's day 1997. There were performances by writer Aidan Dunn, and Dorset poet Ellie McCarthy, who read a healing blessing in verse.

Heathfield Farm off **Heathfield Road** a few hundred yards further on was the summer retreat, *a primitive little farmhouse, three miles from the Church and seven from the butcher's,* of Granville Bradley, Dean of Westminster and friend of Tennyson. He once wrote that, *AT is more worried by his small enemies, the fleas at Farringford, than I like to see him.* Bradley's children played with Tennyson's sons, and his daughter recalled how the two men *roamed the country together, poeticising, botanising, geologising. I can see my father now, a slight, active little figure, armed with a hammer and girt with a capacious knapsack, setting forth joyous as a chamois-hunter, for a day's sport among the fossils of the Isle of Wight cliffs.* It was Bradley who brought his brother-in-law, the music scholar Sir George Grove, editor of the authoritative Dictionary of Music and Musicians, for the first of many visits to Farringford. He in turn was often accompanied by his close friend Sir Arthur Sullivan.

Colwell Road climbs gently to its junction with **Avenue Road** before descending into **Totland.** Peter Giles set his ghost story *A Monster Unto Many* (1980) in the bay here. Most of the action takes place in the old Totland Bay Chalet Hotel, now demolished, and the terrifying denouement occurs on the pier.

> *. . . Dive in. Warm green sea. Round the pier timbers. Powerful swirling and pulling in several directions. But always downwards. Towering steamer. Darkness. I'll be crushed. Salt froth, seaweed, floating things, bits of raft. Then giant paddles reach to chop me, suck me too.*

The hero sees his dead son drowning.

> *fair head like a sea anemone, open eyes like marbles*

The young W H Auden spent Easter 1917 on holiday at Totland Bay with his parents. Newspaper baron Lord Northcliffe once lived in a house on the **Turf Walk.**

At the junction of **Eden Road** with **Cliff Road** lies Wilmington, once the summer residence of Violet Hammersley, a close friend of the Bloomsbury Group (1905-1906). *Rosamond Lehmann's Album* (1985) prints a photograph of the painter Duncan Grant with Mrs Hammersley, sitting together in the window seat. Wilmington was originally a substantial three-storey Victorian house but the upper two floors were removed by Violet so she would be able to see Hurst Castle from Heatherwood, her then home on the Island. It is a magical place with ornate decoration and glass verandahs, one of which contains a fresco by Grant in which a tomboyish girl plays with a bunch of grapes.

I was shown this one evening in late Summer by Violet's son Christopher, a true gentleman of the old school, and a schoolfriend of Aldous Huxley (1894-1963) who occasionally visited here.

Wilmington in **Totland Bay** — The summer residence of Violet Hammersley. Originally three storeys, the upper two were removed so that she could see Hurst Castle from Heatherwood.

As Rosamond Lehmann wrote of Grant and Violet

> *He painted frescos and a portrait of her at her home in Totland Bay. They became devoted to one another. Violet was one of my mother's closest friends, and I spent many happy hours with her. There is a long description of her in 'The Swan in the Evening'.*

Francis Spalding's biography of Grant states that in 1937, *Duncan paid his first visit to Mrs Hammersley's home at Wilmington, perceiving the Island's charms through sea drizzle when she took him for a drive.* The portrait was subsequently bought by Southampton Art Gallery for twenty-five guineas, and can still be seen there. It bears out Rosamond's pen portrait:

> *I believed Violet to be a witch: I feared she might change me or bewitch my mother . . . that elegance of hers in the high Spanish style. Her low-toned intensity in conversation troubled me, as did that hooded, sombre gaze which seemed to me literally to put out tentacles. When she played the piano, the energy and vehemence of her attack made me feel quite faint. Tonight she has flung a black lace mantilla over her raven's wing hair; the rest of her is white satin gleaming against crimson cushions. Looking back, I see that there was none of Beauties' daughters with a magic like hers, nor one in whom so much wit, wisdom, lovingness, forgivingness, strove with such autocratic failings.*

Violet Hammersley was born in the same room (in the British Embassy in Paris) and on the same day as W Somerset Maugham, who inscribed many books to her personally, as did L P Hartley, author of *The Go-Between,* Julian and Juliet Huxley, Rosamond and John Lehmann, Nancy Mitford, Diana Mosley, Robin Maugham, J B Priestley, and Hester Thackeray Fuller, all frequent visitors to Wilmington. Violet had previously lived in Marlow, by the Thames, on which she and her banker husband kept a Venetian *sandalo,* complete with a gondolier called Guilio. As a youth she had her portrait painted by John Singer Sargent (1856-1925). Widowed when young she became a Catholic. She had many quirks, including an inability to travel alone in taxis. She also made a selection from, and translation of, Mme de Sévigne's letters, published with an Introduction by Somerset Maugham in 1955. Violet died at a home for the elderly in London in 1964. The Lehmanns were neighbours on the Thames and her godson, the poet and editor John Lehmann, wrote in his autobiography, *The Whispering Gallery* (1957) that,

> *... after the (Great) war, we went again to stay with the Hammersleys, who had taken a little house at the end of the Turf Walk, and modelled it into the perfect seaside home. By that time Totland Bay had already become a half-buried history of childhood . . . Her children, tall Christopher with the look of a romantic Italian nobleman, mischievous David with whom I was later at Eton and my own special intimate, Monica, the youngest, were our constant playmates.*

But it was another Christopher about whom Lehmann wrote in *Christopher Isherwood: A Personal Memoir* (1987),

> *One of the first things Christopher did was to drive down with me to the Isle of Wight, where my mother was staying in Violet's Totland Bay house while Violet was away in France. That corner of the Island was full of nostalgic memories for both of us.*
> *Other pictures come to mind with extraordinary vividness: one of him pacing up and down the tiny lawn of Violet's house, with a glimpse of the Solent through the trees, discussing China. Another, of him sitting at the lunch-table, or after dinner in the little drawing room, endlessly lecturing my mother – to her fascination and delight.*

Just a hundred yards or so from Wilmington further up **Eden Road** is Little Eden, a jewel of a house painted an attractive shade of green. John Lehmann's sister, the novelist Rosamond Lehmann (1901- 1990) had a tiny cottage built as a summer retreat on land at the rear. It was designed by David Stokes, Mrs Hammersley's son-in- law, and Rosamond spent part of the Second World War here. In *The Swan in the Evening: Fragments of an Inner Life,* Lehmann wrote,

> *Perhaps the regal auras of Charles I and Queen Victoria still lend the island air a higher vibratory frequency; perhaps the murmuring shade of Alfred, Lord Tennyson still brushes the birds, and the tides; perhaps the vestiges of pre-history scattered over and beneath its turf and chalk and sandstone account for the magical atmosphere of certain woods, downs, valleys, chines, and standing stones.*

This strange and beautiful book, its title taken from the folksong 'She Moved Through the Fair', deals, like Peter Giles' novel, with the death of a child. Here, though, the account is autobiographical, not fictional. Rosamond hears the news of the death of her

Little Eden in **Totland** — Novelist Rosamond Lehmann originally had this tiny cottage built as a summer retreat.

daughter Sally while in Totland, and recalls a boat trip long ago to Hurst Castle when Sally was four years old and which almost ended in their both drowning. Lehmann has just been to see her almost completed little house and finds on the terrace a dead young blackbird which had flown straight into the glass front door. She comments, lightly, that this means a death in the family. She returns to the hotel and the news of her daughter's death.

In the Virago reprint of *The Swan in the Evening,* Lehmann recalls sitting on a seat on the Turf Walk, reading the reviews of the first edition. It is as if a circle has been completed.

John Lehmann published some of his sister's short stories in *Penguin New Writing.* One of the most impressive is *The Red-Haired Miss Daintreys,* republished in *The Gypsy's Baby and Other Stories* (1972), in which the novelist meets four sisters while on holiday in Totland, and is based on a childhood memory. At one point in the narrative, she walks alone from the Totland Bay Hotel to nearby Headon Warren, although neither is referred to by name. I find this passage particularly haunting as it describes my own upward plod from Totland village, past my current abode in Cliff Road, and onto National Trust land which leads ultimately to Alum Bay. Everything is different, everything is still the same. Rosamond could only trace these steps now as a ghost. As, some day, will I too.

> *I went out along the turf walk, up the hill past the crazy grey house with turrets and the square red house where a family of public schoolboys in white flannels held perpetual tennis parties beyond cropped weedless*

lawns and beds of begonias, geraniums and; through the pine coppice and out onto the climbing cliff path which led through a place of brambles and gorse bushes to the heathery downs.

Rosamond Lehmann had a post-war affair with C Day-Lewis, the Poet Laureate now buried near to the final resting place of Thomas Hardy's heart, in Stinsford Churchyard, in Dorset. Her poem *The Bay* (1951), revisits the Totland of her childhood, but finds no real consolation in it.

Here the white strand again; no change;
  This gap in time revisited,
The lucent dream, the cryptic shore,
Moon, stars, transparencies once more;
A cryptic dream, the same; and strange;
Time past; time found again; time dead.
  Again these cliffs, this blinding arc
Powdered and silvered, rock embossed . . .

Chine Cliff, my own home therein, a tiny garret overlooking the sea, is in **Cliff Road.** Among the guests to wake up to the sound of the waves here have been the Norfolk folk singer Peter Bellamy who put Kipling's verse to folk music, and the Finnish poet and dramatist Ilpo Tolenon. The artist Julian Bell drew scenes from the window for *Poems from the Island* (1981), and Winchester poet Elizabeth Bewick wrote,

To sleep with the sea's breathing in my ear
surrounded by rich hangings and old books,
shelves crammed to the eyebrows of each room
a miser's hoard of words to glut the mind.

This is the house described by Rosamond Lehmann in the *Red-Haired Miss Daintreys,* though the tennis courts have long ago collapsed into the sea, and the current owner Vic Pettett bravely landscapes what is left, valiantly postponing the inevitable.

I live on the fault-line, high on a cliff-top; my rural fastness
slopes off to the sea. Unsung the landlord tills a vertical garden,
wrested from neglect, a maze of drunken paths, tottering.
  They harden
into serpent paths, winding, through a paradise of builders' rubble, the
waste land reclaimed. Snowdrops surface, like a corpse's stubble.

                              Brian Hinton: The Heart's Clockwork (1989)

Cliff Road leads ultimately to **Headon Hill** which belongs to the National Trust. 'Headon Hill' was also the pseudonym of Francis Edward Granger, who wrote many popular thrillers a hundred or so years ago. A mysterious figure, his books include *The Cliff Path Mystery* and *Spies of the Wight,* packed with local detail. The latter turns on attempts by a German spy ring to obtain the keys to Golden Hill Fort: much of the action takes place in Totland and Alum Bay, where the hero is thrown down a well. The escaping spies take to their yacht, but it is blown out of the water by a single shot from the Hatherwood Battery, sited (one assumes) on **Hatherwood Point.** One vital clue is found at the Lending Library and Reading Room on Totland beach, *a resort dotted up and down on either side of a gently sloping chine, some half a hundred pretty houses, from whose leafy* *gardens came the merry voices of young men and maidens playing tennis.* Recently restored, the Reading Room is now a waterfront restaurant.

Just off **Alum Bay Old Road** as it winds up from Totland lies Swallow House. Formerly known as The Links because of the golf course in which it once sat, the house also has claims to less tangible connections. Between the wars, it was the centre for Gurdjieff's strange philosophy, and attracted the young theatre director, Peter Brook.

In 1917, W H Auden on a visit to **Alum Bay,** was fascinated by a strange building on top of the cliffs. To his parent's horror it subsequently turned out to be an isolation hospital for infectious diseases. Its foundations still remain. Edward Thomas (1878-1917) opens his survey of the Island by quoting an anonymous poet who had published an account, in three quite dreadful cantos of his visit.

> *Now wafted slowly by the indented shore*
> *With panting heart the Needles we explore*

The 17th century traveller, Celia Fiennes (1662-1741) reported that

> *The Needles are severall Great Rocks, craggy, and severall stand out in the sea which makes it very hazardous for shipps to pass there especially in a Storme, or for strangers, the passage being narrow between the Needles and Hurst Castle can easily command any ship that would pass there.*

The young Charlotte Mew (1869-1928) noted how

> *past the white points of the Needles, over the Island sea, the pigeons of woods and other worlds flock home in autumn, dashing themselves somehow at the end of the journey against the pane of St Catherine's Light, dropping dazed and spent on the wet sand.*

A trip to the Needle's lighthouse inspired Rudyard Kipling's short story *The Disturber of Traffic,* first published in 1891.

> *Of the English south-coast Lights, that of St-Cecilia-Under-The-Cliff is the most powerful, for it guards a very foggy coast. When the sea- mist veils all, St Cecilia turns a hooded head to the sea and sings a song of two words once every minute. From the land that song resembles the bellowing of a brazen bull; but offshore they understand, and the steamers grunt gratefully in answer.*

The poet, Sean Street, wrote much the same, after a night kept awake in my clifftop flat in Totland by this same 'low hooting',

> *From deep, deep beneath its waves,*
> *strange monstrous one-eyed fish moaned*
> *their cries the texture of sad wool.*

A Walk in Winter (1989)

In Kipling's story, once the lighthouseman has told his strange tale, daylight dawns to reveal a scene topographically halfway between The Needles and St Catherine's lighthouse at Niton.

*The sea fog rolled back from the cliffs in trailed wreaths and dragged
patches, as the sun rose and made the dead sea alive and splendid. A
lark went up from the cliffs behind St Cecilia, and we smelt a smell of
cows in the lighthouse pasture below.*

Richard J Hutchings revived in print a three-handed 'extemporare sonnet' by Alfred
Tennyson, James White and Edmund Peel about a boat trip round the Needles in 1846.
Almost certainly the first visit by the future Poet Laureate to the West Wight and a scene
which had already inspired the young William Turner to attempt his first painting in oils.
The three writers combine to produce a round robin of a poem, like master
instrumentalists each in turn picking up a tune.

Tennyson	*Two poets and a mighty dramatist*
	Threaded the Needles on a day in June:
	Upon the ocean hung a lucid mist,
	And round the cliffs the seabird's plaintive tune
	Resounded as they rowed beneath the sun;
Peel	*But Nature is a woundrous harmonist:*
	And as the boat the gentle waters kissed,
Tennyson	*The long wave sparkled in the sleepy noon,*
	Strong was the glare on that o'er arching chalk,
	And soft the washing of the summer seas;
	And deep and thoughtful was the poets' talk,
Peel	*The mighty dramatist lounging at ease;*
	And all those three great spirits, not to balk
	Their aspirations, clamour'd Bread and Cheese!

Sir Thomas Noon Talfourd (1795-1854) composed *Lines Written at the Needles Hotel,
Alum Bay* in praise of the famous coloured sands patterning the cliffs. Its only claim to
fame is that it contains one of the longest sentences in the English poetic canon!

> *. . . From the gate*
> *Of this home-featured Inn, which nestling cleaves*
> *To its own shelf among the downs, begirt*
> *With trees which lift no branches to defy*
> *The fury of the storm, but crouch in love*
> *Round the low snow-white walls whence they receive*
> *More shelter than they lend – the heart-soothed guest*
> *Views a furze-dotted common, on each side*
> *Wreathed into waving eminences, clothed*
> *Above the furze with scanty green, in front*
> *Indented sharply to admit the sea,*
> *Spread thence in softest blue, – to which a gorge*
> *Sinking within the valley's deepening green*
> *Invites by grassy path; the Eastern down*
> *Swelling with pride into the waters, shows*
> *Its sward-tipped precipice of radiant white,*
> *And claims the dazzling peak beneath its brow*
> *Part of its ancient bulk, which hints the strength*

Of those famed Pinnacles that still withstand
The conquering waves.

William Allingham visited Alum Bay with Tennyson, in a particularly depressed condition – *England is going down.* In 1863, on a walk with poet and anthologist Francis Turner Palgrave, Allingham records *the coloured cliffs, smeary in effect, like something spilt.* A more recent visitor, the scientist Nigel Calder, describes how *the morning shadows subdue the multiple colours of Alum Bay, but even so you can see the streaks of upended sandstone in narrow bands of white, black, yellow, green, red, pink and brown.*

From Alum Bay, a steep path leads up to Tennyson's memorial, a Celtic cross made of Cornish granite, set at the highest point of the chalk down, 483 feet above sea level. A later poet Laureate, Sir John Betjeman, described this walk as being like *a strange and terrifyng dream.*

The Tennyson Monument on Tennyson Down was dedicated in 1897 to replace an old wooden beacon, used as a kind of visitor's book. Its supports, and even the nearby turf were cut and carved with the names of the poet's admirers. The new monument was engraved more formally: *this cross is raised, a Beacon to Sailors, by the people of Freshwater and other friends in England and America.* The ashes of noted Tennyson scholar Richard J Hutchings (1922-1991) were scattered here at sunset.

November dawns and dewy-glooming downs,
The gentle shower, the smell of dying leaves,
And the low moan of leaden-coloured seas.

Tennyson: Enoch Arden (1864)

It was up on these windswept slopes that the poet wrote *The Charge of the Light Brigade,* having read in the London 'Times' that morning, 2nd December 1854, that 'someone had blundered', and this was the origin of the metre of his poem. In fact it wasn't. The reporter actually wrote of 'some hideous blunder', but this must have transformed itself in the poet's mind as he climbed up from Farringford. Thus does true genius work!

Alfred was morbidly shy, and once ran away from a flock of sheep, thinking them to be a crowd of admirers. Indeed, towards the end of his life, the Poet Laureate would be followed by a weird procession of the reverential and the curious, as he pushed Emily about in her wheelchair.

He had hacked a series of uneven steps out of the turf where it became steep, *cut with Tennyson's own hand, so that without undue exertion she might share his favourite walk.* The air up here was, he declared, worth *sixpence a pint.* It could also take on a life of its own. Anne Thackeray walked on High Down *while gulls came sideways flashing their white breasts against the edge of the cliff, and the Poet's cloak flapped time to the gusts of the west wind.* Such weather suited Tennyson's inner storms, subjugated into verse, and allied to meticulous observation of nature. In his *Autobiography,* Bayard Taylor recalls Alfred as . . .

a man tall and broad-shouldered, with hair, beard and eyes of southern darkness. We reached the steep combe of the chalk cliff and slowly wandered westward until we reached the Needles. During the conversation with which we beguiled the way, I was struck with the variety of the Poet's knowledge. Not a little flower on the Down which

*the sheep had spared escaped his notice, and the geology of the coast,
both terrestrial and submarine, was perfectly familiar to him.*

As Hester Fuller reported, *walks were the custom at Farringford,* and the poet would daily take the same route, up onto High Down and back, whatever the weather or time of the year. Tennyson's ghost, dressed in cloak and wideawake hat, is said to appear up here on each anniversary of his birthday, 6th August 1809.

Steep steps lead down to the **High Down Inn,** once a haunt of local smugglers. Just off a sharp bend in the road at this point, the drive of Weston Manor can be seen. Once the home of W G Ward, friend of Tennyson and writer on religious subjects, the Ward family also owned Northwood House in Cowes. W G Ward was Tennyson's neighbour from 1870 to 1882, though he visited the West Wight frequently in the 1860s and was introduced to the poet by Dean Bradley. The poet Alfred Noyes (1880-1959) described W G Ward as *the Catholic Dr Johnson. I like to think of him approaching the priests, at the end of an elaborate service in his sumptuous private chapel, with the solemn whisper 'nunc est bibendum'. Now for a drink.* Tennyson's niece, Agnes Weld recalls that

> *from the field at the south side of Hawkridge to Weston Manor House, on the opposite hill, wound a special gravel path, made for his own use by the Squire of Weston Manor, known as 'Ideal Ward' because of his book 'The Ideal of a Christian Church' which caused him the loss of his fellowship at Oxford. He was at one time President of the Metaphysical Society, of which Tennyson was a member, and in whose formation Professor Pritchard had a share, and both men were equally ardent students of philosophy, and had in common a perfectly guileless child-like nature. The mixture of the dreamy student and the hearty friend in Mr Ward was very amusing, for his carriage had generally half passed by before he discovered that a lady had bowed to him, and then he would spring up as if shot, turn right round, and bow effusively, hat in hand.*

Squire Ward had the house built when forced to resign holy orders because of his conversion to Catholicism. Pioneer photographer Julia Cameron would load a donkey cart up with photographic equipment and come to the Manor to work, although the results do not appear to have survived.

Ward's son, Wilfred, later described the West Wight of the 1860s as *seething with intellectual life. The Poet* (Tennyson, who else?) *was, of course its centre, and that remarkable woman Mrs Cameron was stage manager.*

The Ward family now lies buried next to Alfred Noyes in St Saviour's churchyard, Totland.

Weston Manor is now a home for men with learning difficulties, helping to bring them back into the community. Ward's beneficial influence lingers on. D H Lawrence's early novel *The Trespasser* (1912) contains scenes which draw on his own holiday memories. Here the doomed lovers walk past the church, on their way back from Alum Bay to Freshwater.

> *The way home lay across country, through deep little lanes where the late foxgloves sat seriously, like sad hounds; over open downlands*

rough with gorse and ling, and through pocketed hollows of bracken and trees. They came to a small Roman Catholic church in the fields. There the carved Christ looked down on the dead whose sleeping forms made mounds under the coverlet. The path skirted the churchyard wall, so that she had on one hand the sleeping dead, and on the other, Sigmund, strong and vigorous . . . she rested on him like a bird on a swaying bough.

Where Alum Bay Old Road becomes **Moon's Hill,** two of the cottages on the left, known formerly as Farm Cottages but now renamed Middleton Farm Cottages, have the Tennysons' initials engraved over their porches, and above their downstairs windows. As George Napier writes, *returning from the Needles, we at once know when we are within the marches of the Poet's estate from the many neat little cottages peeping out amid bowers of honeysuckle, with a monogram of the letters AET – Alfred and Emily Tennyson, entwined – cut in a red stone over the doorway.*

Middleton Farm Cottages, Moons Hill — Freshwater with the initials of Tennyson and his wife over the porch and downstairs windows.

Agnes Weld adds how she watched her uncle construct these carvings.

He had an artist's eye for form, and would lay an ivy spray by his side, and carve a faithful copy of its graceful outlines; and the design for this, together with an Agnus Dei, to which he had taken a great fancy, formed the decorative terracotta mouldings round the windows of a model

15

labourer's cottage on his estate, whose erection he used to superintend daily.

Tennyson was an advanced thinker for his time. *Labourer's homes, each a nest in bloom,* as he wrote in *Enoch Arden.* He wished the tenants on his estate to live well, rather than in tumbledown, rat infested hovels, to which the watercolours of Helen Allingham now add a spurious charm.

Hereabouts once stood The Briary, where painter and sculptor G F Watts (1817-1904) built a studio, and brought his child bride, the actress Ellen Terry (1847-1928). His good friends, Sara (Julia Margaret Cameron's sister), Val and May Prinsep from Little Holland House in London often stayed. Val painted his sister May on High Down and Hallam Tennyson fell in love with her. Years later she became the third Lady Tennyson.

The Briary, which was built in 1873 and stood at the foot of Tennyson Down, was so called because of the profusion of wild roses in the area. Laura Troubridge later eulogised the magical summer holidays that she had spent in *a three storied building in red and white, half villa, half cottage, wholly delightful.* In those days before the railway came to Freshwater, bringing day trippers and a building boom, *an exquisite peace brooded over that part of the Island. Nightingales sang in the copse at the back of The Briary. There were leafy glades formed by tall trees whose branches reached overhead; soft, blustering winds brought the tang of the sea to the garden, which was full of old fashioned flowers, lavender and sweet geranium, and climbing white and yellow roses.*

Agnes Weld remembered Tennyson's daily visits to chat with

> *old Thoby Prinsep, who has all the mien and manner befitting the post of Director of the East India Company which he held so long. Though the eyesight had long gone, yet his mind was full of vigour, and he could converse by the hour with my uncle on politics, literature, science, or theology, for his ready grasp of every imaginable subject was only less wonderful than his marvellous memory . . .*

Watts' marriage to Ellen Terry lasted only a matter of months. His second wife, Mary, was made of sterner stuff, though in *Annals of a Painter's Life* (1912) her attitude is one of pure worship at her 'Signor'. He had been down at Farringford, while Mary Watts spent the morning with Alice Liddell in wonderland, under a big elm on The Briary lawn.

> *When one o'clock came we went to meet the party. We had just climbed the little rise that led to a broad green glade when the three came in sight. Down the great aisle of elms (Alas, lost in the 70s!), there came a white Russian deerhound flashing like silver through the sun or shade, and the central figure of the Poet, a note of black in the midst of the vivid green, grand in the folds of his ample cloak, and his face looming grandly from the shadow of the giant hat. 'Monumental', Signor would call him.*

> *As we went towards The Briary, the teeming life of nature seemed to turn their thoughts to a life beyond this life. Lord Tennyson quoted with regret the saddest epitaph he knew, written by a friend who had no belief in the future, and then with moistening eyes he gave us the*

16

triumphant words placed over a woman's grave: 'I have loved, I love, I shall love'. But given in the terse Latin, 'Amavi, Amo, Amabo'.

Mary also recounts Mrs Prinsep hosting a family party with the *beautiful young widow,* her niece Mrs Herbert Duckworth. This was Julia Jackson, who later remarried. Her second husband was the Victorian scholar Sir Leslie Stephen (1832-1904) whose most noteworthy achievement was his editorship of the *Dictionary of National Biography* between 1871 and 1882. The daughters of this second marriage were to grow up into Vanessa Bell the painter and Virginia Woolf the novelist, twin pillars of the Bloomsbury group. Julia herself was the model for the gracious, much admired Mrs Ramsey in *To the Lighthouse* (1927).

In *Three Freshwater Friends* (1933/1992), Hester Thackeray Fuller describes The Briary in its full glory, *the smiling lawns and terraces, the clipped yew hedges, and the great magnolia tree which covers the front of the house.* Fuller captures the memories of those who knew The Briary in its prime: *in those days how full of noble thought and inspiration the house was, and tradition still speaks of the very remarkable set of people who lived there.* The Briary was virtually destroyed by fire in 1934.

From **Briary Lane** to **Freshwater Bay** along **Bedbury Lane** is only a mile or so and on the way lies Farringford, for many years the home of the greatest poet of the Victorian age, Alfred, Lord Tennyson (1809-1892), the Poet Laureate.

In October 1853, he had been staying with the Reverend James White in Bonchurch and went to see Farringford, and *found it looking rather wretched, with wet leaves trampled into the lawn.* Later that month, he brought over Emily, whom he had married three years before.

> *The railway did not go further than Brockenhurst then, and the steamer felt itself in no way bound to wait for the omnibus which brought as many of the passengers as it could from the train. We crossed in a rowing boat. It was a still November evening. One dark heron flew over the Solent backed by a daffodil sky.*
>
> Journal of Emily Tennyson, 1853

Standing in the drawing room and looking down to Freshwater Bay, Emily decided that *I must have that view,* and so they did. Emily's *Journal* records their attempt to create Eden here, surrounding the house with thick hedges, planting gardens – Alfred would mow the lawns at midnight – while bringing up their two young sons, Hallam and Lionel.

And here it was to be that Tennyson wrote *Maud* (1855), *Enoch Arden* (1864), *Idylls of the King* (1872) and the touching invitation *The Revd F D Maurice* (1855). The Island becomes a place of sanctuary from the doctrinal wars then raging, a refuge, a place of peace.

> *Where, far from noise and smoke of town*
> *I watch the twilight falling brown*
> *All round a careless-ordered garden*
> *Close to the ridge of a noble down.*
>
> *You'll have no scandal while you dine,*
> *But honest talk and wholesome wine,*

An engraving of **Farringford** as the house was some fifty years before the Tennysons

Farringford in the present from the approach road

And only hear the magpie gossip
Garrulous under a roof of pine:

For groves of pine on either hand,
To break the blast of winter, stand;
And further on, the hoary Channel
Tumbles a breaker on chalk and sand.

Not everyone found it so hospitable. When the Tennysons moved into their new home in November 1853, *it was a misty morning, & two of the servants on seeing it burst into tears saying they could never live in such a lonely place.* The house, a masterpiece of revived Gothic, was built around 1800, near the site of the original Prior's Manor, which belonged to the Abbey of Lyra, in Normandy. Some of the field names, Prior's Field, Maiden's Croft, still refer back to this time.

Tennyson became a firm friend of Sir John Simeon, the jovial squire of Swainston Manor on the Calbourne Road, near Newport. When Simeon found four lines of verse in the poet's study, he was so taken by them that he suggested Tennyson expand them into a much longer work.

O! that 'twere possible
After long grief and pain
To find the arms of my true love
Round me once again

The result was *Maud,* although some reviewers suggested that the poem would be better described as Mad or Mud. Nevertheless, it was largely with the profits from it that Tennyson was able to purchase Farringford outright.

For Alfred Church,

The house, while not possessing any architectural pretensions, has something singularly attractive about it. Creeping plants clothe it from roof-tree to foundation with a mantle of green. A delightful garden laid out by the poet and his wife, surrounds it, and beyond this again is a small, well-wooded park. Both park and house are sheltered from the south-westerly gales by a ridge of down.

The house commands fine views down to the Bay, and across the Solent. Tennyson's grandson Lionel, in *From Verse to Worse,* records the house as being built *on the side of a steep knoll that was formerly the site of one of the many Telegraph Stations which were used in the 18th century for communication by semaphore.* In the poet's own time, he would signal across to Aubrey House in Keyhaven, where Emily's ageing parents had recently moved, by a system of flags.

Here, indeed, was an earthly paradise. As Emily wrote to Julia Margaret Cameron, *Alfred has been reading Hamlet to me, and since then has been down to the Bay by the loud voice of the sea. There is something so wholesome in beauty . . . all we have here in those delicate tints of a distant Bay and the still more distant headlands.*

One of Alfred's favourite walks was across **Green Lane** (at what is now called **Tennyson's Bridge**) and up to the Down that bears his name. Here he was content with manageable horizons, *chaining fancy now at home/among the quarried downs of Wight.* First there was a problem to be, literally, overcome.

A right of way extends through this part of his estate, nor was there any escape, for the public path ran directly across all the convenient avenues to the sea. But the law, though it forbids the stoppage of a right of way, has nothing to say of its altitude. So one day Tennyson set to work, and by lowering the level of the lane where it crossed the path he chose for his daily walks, neatly and entirely outwitted his enemies.

Arthur Paterson: The Homes and Haunts of Tennyson

The waiting public would see only the brief flash of the poet's hat and cloak, as with head bent he sprinted across the bridge, and so to freedom. He also built a wooden summer house on the edge of the estate, painting crescent moons on its walls by hand. *Being a great worker with his hands, he painted the forms of dragons and strange monsters.* From here, Tennyson could watch and hear the waves breaking on the beach at nearby Freshwater Bay.

All by myself in my own dark garden ground,
Listening now to the tide in its broad-flung shipwrecking roar
Now to the scream of a madden'd beach dragg'd down by the wave
Walk'd in a wintry wind by a ghastly glimmer, and found
The shining daffodil dead, and Orion low in his grave.

Maud

Hallam Tennyson recalled how his father would walk up and down in front of this summer house on starlit nights, and thus *lines and great thoughts would come to him.* Agnes Weld records his amusement, rather than annoyance, at holidaymakers who used to steal his quill pens from here, leaving the *moultings of some barn-door fowl* in their place.

Arthur Paterson completes the history. *The arbour was preserved exactly as Tennyson had built and decorated it, until one day it was found that tourists like veritable 'body- snatchers' had torn away every vestige of the paintings, leaving the place a wrecked and empty shell. Now the bare walls and beams, which even vandalism could not steal, are all that remain. Rank grass grows about the bolted door, and the place is as deserted as last year's nest.*

William Allingham recalls a summer evening at Farringford: they were sitting after dinner in the drawing room, with its magnificent view of Afton Down rising like the prow of a giant ship from the Bay. Tennyson reproved his sons for their cruelty. *Why cut short the butterflies' lives. What are we? We ourselves are the merest moths. Look at that hill, it is four hundred million years old. Think of that! Let the moths have their little lives.* Agnes Weld remembers Alfred pointing out

the lake-like expanse of Freshwater Bay, its Mediterranean blue waters chequered with streaks of rosy pink, bordered by white and red coloured cliffs, which gleam like some tropical flower.

Tennyson's original study was in the attic, a tiny room with one window looking out to the lawn. His friends would climb steep wooden steps up to this 'fumitory'. Agnes Weld remembers Charles Kingsley, author of *The Water Babies,* who *here talked on all sorts of topics and walked up and down for hours smoking furiously, and affirming that tobacco was the only thing which kept his nerves quiet.*

Other famous visitors to Farringford included Charles Tennyson Turner, the poet's brother and a fine poet in his own right, Henry Wadsworth Longfellow, author of *Hiawatha,* who called in 1868, Edward Fitzgerald, Francis Palgrave, editor of the *Golden Treasury,* William Barnes, the Dorset dialect writer, Algernon Swinburne, a fraught meeting this, and Edward Lear who would perform his nonsense verse to his own piano accompaniment.

William Allingham, Lewis Carroll, Arthur Hugh Clough, music historian Sir George Groves, Oliver Wendell Holmes, Benjamin Jowett, Coventry Patmore, and the American poet Bayard Taylor: all came to meet the great man.

The guest list was not confined to his fellow authors. Painters who called included Holman Hunt, Sir John Millais, George Du Maurier and Kate Greenaway. Scientists included Charles Darwin, the botanist Granville Bradley, John Tyndall, and Sir John Herschel, the Astronomer Royal and one of the inventors of photography. There were more: Guiseppe Garibaldi, the Italian patriot and guerrilla general, Prince Albert, husband and cousin of Queen Victoria and Jenny Lind the 'Swedish nightingale'.

A typical visit is that recorded by Lewis Carroll (Charles Dodgson) in April 1859, who first refutes the idea that he went to Freshwater merely to seek out the Laureate. He finds Alfred *mowing his lawn in a wideawake hat and spectacles. I had to introduce myself as he is too short-sighted to recognise people.* Invited to dinner, Dodgson is taken over to the house to see some pictures, including Tennyson's own photographic experiments, and meets Hallam in the nursery, *who remembered me more readily than his father had done.* There are *two hours of interesting talk* in Tennyson's smoking room at the very top of the house, a conversation in which the great poet is instigator and referee.

> *Tennyson told me that often on going to bed after being engaged in composition he had dreamed long passages of poetry. ('You, I suppose', turning to me, 'dream photographs')*
>
> Herbert Gernsheim: Lewis Carroll – Photographer (1949)

The next day, Dodgson takes round a photographic album, which Emily and the boys peruse with delight, Lionel *insisting on reading out the poetry opposite the pictures.* When they come to their father's portrait, Lionel begins boldly *'The Pope', on which Mrs Tennyson began laughing, and Tennyson growled from the other end of the table,'Hollo! What's this about the Pope?' but no one ventured to explain the allusion.* One senses Tennyson as one might a caged lion, indulged but feared by his wife and sons, liable to turn nasty without warning at any moment, but kind at heart and full of intellectual energy. Not a man for small talk, and a stimulating but somewhat wearing host.

Thomas Edison visited Tennyson at Farringford to immortalise the poet's voice on wax cylinders. Not an easy task, for he was an immensely shy man. Emily hung a whistle round her neck which she would blow whenever unexpected visitors arrived. This warning would enable Alfred to make good his escape down the secret spiral staircase built into a corner of his new study. From there he would flee under the overhanging vines, past the magnolia tree brought from America, and along the 'primrose path of dalliance'. This was the family name for the path that leads out to the rustic bridge and thence into the Wilderness.

Tennyson loved the flowers and could not bear to see any plucked, even when growing in profusion in the fields . . . the copse on Maiden's Croft was full of bluebells.

Arthur Paterson: The Homes of Tennyson (1905)

George Napier described the park which surrounds the house. *No stiff stone wall encloses, but a high natural bank, surmounted by a hedge. Here and there a gap in the 'wall of green' lays bare to view the park, charmingly varied with clusters of large trees and deep pasture.* The gardener's lodge stands not within the park, but opposite the entrance in **Bedbury Lane,** while the park itself is now a miniature golf course, with a small island surrounded by a lake at its centre.

Alfred and Emily laid out the grounds, and the poet took great delight in pointing out to the novelist Oliver Wendell Holmes *the finest and rarest of his trees. Everything grows with such a lavish extravagance of green. I felt as if weary eyes and over-tasked brains might reach their happiest haven of rest.* Trimly kept corridors, with a rampart of the *dry tongued laurel* on either side led to a large walled garden, with figs growing outside and a profusion of rose bushes, just like in Maud. The upper lawn behind the house, was *half lawn, half woodland glade. The grass was soft and fine showing no rankness.* Here Tennyson and friends would sit out on sunny afternoons. Alfred created a kitchen garden, with an arbour for Emily, with bushes of white lilac on either side: no wonder that with *its fine old walls, which may have stood since the monks of Lyra Abbey walked there, this was my favourite haunt.*

As caught in words, the place seems wreathed in an eternal Summer, a jewel in the crown of Empire. Anne Thackeray had taken long walks with Tennyson, and his acute eye informed hers, and thus her prose.

> *The firebrand in the still rippled sea turned from flame to silver as the light changed and ebbed. The light on the sea seemed dimmer, but then the land caught fire in turn and trees and downs and distant rooftops blazed in this great illumination.*
>
> Anne Thackeray: From An Island (1880)

Thirty years later, D H Lawrence caught this same sense of an alien world, but now tinged with the sinister.

> *The sea was glittering unbearably, like a scaled dragon wreathing. The houses of Freshwater slept, as cattle sleep motionless in the hollow valley. Green Farringford on the slope was drawn over with a shadow of heat and sleep.*
>
> D H Lawrence: The Trespasser (1912)

Ernest Raymond's novel *The Visit of Brother Ives* (1960) conveys the sense of an almost overwhelming benificence. *Tennyson Down is spread with cushions of gorse, their gold so brilliant that it might have been something spilled from the sun.* And this in a book about a murder, no less.

Even while Tennyson was still alive, Farringford was already a signpost on the tourist map: sadly prosaic, drained of its former glories:

At their feet lay pretty woods, noticeable as surrounding the house of our poet Tennyson, a name not unfamiliar to the two elder children, who had already learned some of his poetry, and read much more.

Anonymous: Six Months at Freshwater (1886)

For W H Auden, it was here that wild Tennyson *became a fossil*, and Alfred Noyes was disturbed on moving to the Island in 1929 to receive a telephone call which began 'This is Alfred Tennyson speaking'. It was the poet's grandson, but Noyes found Farringford a mausoleum to match Osborne House.

His library was exactly as he had left it, with his pipe and tobacco on a large writing table, and a curious little stair winding down from the library to the garden, a kind of escape exit that somehow suggested a miniature turret stair in one of the Arthurian idylls.

Alfred Noyes: Two Worlds for Memory (1953)

At its foot stood two bears, carved in wood, which Tennyson had brought home from Switzerland. There was a one-armed bandit standing there when last I visited! The same note of incongruity is struck by the modern poet and close friend of Philip Larkin, Robert Conquest, who visits the *Tennyson and TV Room* to find

– his cloak, his stick, some books. And – ah! –
Grandstand, bright through Gothic gloom

Robert Conquest: 'To Be a Pilgrim', Forays (1979)

Jeremy Hooker literally passes Farringford by, to avoid disappointment.

Was it idolatry or love?
Nettles hide the sign.
Through the heart
of this deep hollow
the road leads on.

Jeremy Hooker: West Wight, Solent Shore (1978)

All is not lost. The poet's study now plays host to the Farringford Tennyson Society, as well as to Grandstand. David Gascoyne, Andrew Motion and Sean Street have read their poetry there, while Ann Thwaite gave a preview of her biography of Emily Tennyson, and Michael Thorn an after-taste of his controversial life of Alfred. In 1987, Virginia Woolf's satire *Freshwater* received its first open air production on Emily's terrace – Elizabeth Hutchings played a particularly regal Queen Victoria – with Professors Philip Collins and Brian Southam among the audience.

Tennyson is now part of the media world. John Betjeman filmed here, in love with both the poet and his house, *it is a long Georgian building in a sweet and fancy Gothic style of the period, a good deal older than Tennyson.* Former Goon, Sir Harry Secombe, brought his Highway television show here, with the actor Anthony Bate reading *Ring Out Wild Bells* straight to camera. Among the many set pieces of the comic novel *Tennyson's Gift* is high tea at Farringford, with Emily desperately finding and then destroying a dozen copies of a review of Enoch Arden in the *Westminster Quarterly,* which Julia Cameron has hidden all over the house and garden. Emily finds it under the carpet, on the stairs to the library, inside one of Alfred's shoes, nailed to the trunk of a Wellingtonia, in the poet's hat – into which she vomits, so that is the end of that copy!

> *Emily smiled at her guests, 'It must have been a joke', she explained. Alfred spluttered, 'Well if it was, it's the first one you've ever made'.*
>
> Lynn Truss: Tennyson's Gift (1996)

Alfred finds the last copy though, baked in a pie. It is all too much for Emily: *her skinny body fell to the grass, twitched once, and lay still.* The author of this 'entertainment', albeit one researched with meticulous care is the TV critic of the *Times*, and the book is paced and structured like a film. Indeed, various filmscripts are currently circulating, based on the Farringford circle, some purely comic, some mysterious and odd.

The most extraordinary of these must surely be *A Glass House*, by Kriv Stenders and Billy MacKinnon, who co-wrote the movie *Small Faces*. That was set among the tenements of Glasgow: this script is closer in spirit to *The Piano*, on which MacKinnon also worked and creates a melancholy, violent, strange miasma, half historical, half invented. Through the gloom, Alfred Tennyson and Julia Cameron conduct a thwarted love affair. Brenda Blethwyn and John Hurt have already agreed to play these two roles.

The ancestor of all such recreations is Virginia Woolf's play *Freshwater*, written in 1923, first performed in 1935, and eventually published in 1976. Set in Dimbola and at the Needles, with Farringford an offstage presence, the two surviving versions of this private bonbon are a kind of jaunty counterpart of Lytton Strachey's *Eminent Victorians*, mocking the high seriousness of the age, with affection and a certain silliness. This was, after all, keeping things in the family!

> *Ellen Terry:*   *Tell me, Mr Tennyson, have you ever picked primroses in a lane?*
> *Tennyson:*   *Scores of times.*
> *Ellen:*   *And did Lady Tennyson ever jump over your head on a horse?*
> *Tennyson:*   *Emily jump? Emily jump? She has lain on her sofa for fifty years, and I should be surprised, nay I should be shocked, if she ever got up again.*
> *Ellen:*   *Then I suppose you were never in love. Nobody ever jumped over your head and dropped a white rose into your hand and galloped away.*
> *Tennyson:*   *My life has been singularly free from amorous excitement of the kind you describe. Tell me more.*

The first performance of *Freshwater* was at 8 Fitzroy Square in London, in Vanessa Bell's studio, Bloomsbury's epicentre. Duncan Grant played George Watts, with Leonard Woolf and Angelica Bell, and Vanessa playing her own great aunt. Something in the play, perhaps its loving mockery of the idea of a life devoted to art, has attracted celebrities not otherwise known for their dramatic talents. Later performances of Woolf's play have included the poet Heathcote Williams in a one-off production at the Royal Court directed by Ann Jellicoe, and a successful run at a small theatre opposite Camden's Roundhouse. A 1983 production played entirely in French featured the playwright Eugene Ionesco, film director Alain Robbe-Grillet, and novelist Nathalie Sarraute, fierce modernists all. A 1986 production in Texas featured Quentin Bell, Margaret

Drabble – as the maid Mary Magdalen! – and narration by Robert Hardy. Lynn Redgrave played Ellen Terry.

Memories of Tennyson continue to weave their spell. As Joseph Chiari recalls, *T S Eliot was not a man of low grounds or plains, he was a man of heights . . . he pulled you up at once to his level, and walked side by side with you, as we did on the cliff at Freshwater, talking about Tennyson.* Poet J J Lumsden still lives locally. He retraces the poet's steps

> *pass the duckpond and the fair-way,*
> *ashen stumps you knew as elms,*
> *Linger by the Primrose Walk you loved.*
>
> R J Lumsden: The Beachcomber and the Swan (1990)

Mrs Thackeray Ritchie remembered that Farringford, *seemed like a charmed place, with green walls without, and speaking walls within. There hung Dante with his solemn nose and wreath; Italy gleamed over the doorways; friend's faces lined the passages, books filled the shelves, and a glow of crimson was everywhere; the oriel drawing-room window was full of green and golden leaves, of the sound of birds and the distant sea.*

Locals took a more sanguine view of the famous poet in their midst. A lady who called on Tennyson's shepherd in his retirement, expressed her admiration of his former master as a poet.

> *"You would never think he was one if you heard him talk" replied the old man. "At any rate he has a good and noble face", continued the astonished visitor. "You would not think so if you looked at him" persisted her host*

The growing incursion of uninvited visitors, the 'cockneys' who came to gawp at him, led to Alfred building a summer retreat, Aldworth, in Surrey. It was there that he died, having written *Crossing the Bar* on his final visit to the Island. Farringford is now an hotel, Tennyson's first study a guest bedroom, his second the TV lounge and home to the Farringford Tennyson Society. Green Lane still runs behind the house as a public footpath, under the rustic bridge which leads to The Wilderness, and on to the Home Farm, so often painted by Helen Allingham.

In 1970, Britt Ekland joined Hayley Mills and Hywel Bennett at Farringford. The hotel provided both accommodation and location for a film version of Agatha Christie's *Endless Night,* released the following year.

Farringford Farm was known as Home Farm by Tennyson, and was much painted by Helen Allingham, wife of the poet William Allingham. Her early watercolours appeared under the name of Helen Paterson illustrating such volumes as *The Cottage Homes of England* (1909) and draw largely on the picturesque but decaying farm buildings of Freshwater. Helen's particular genius was to see beauty in what previous artists had taken to be scenes of deprivation and squalor. It is largely due to her that such buildings have survived to become protected monuments: **Middleton** is now a conservation area, and God help anyone who puts up a television aerial or fits double glazing without permission from the local Council. There can be no doubt that Mrs Allingham painted in soft focus, but she also meticulously recorded the holes in the roof.

Her book illustrations were part of a larger process of repatriation. George Napier comments, quoting Tennyson, that

> Home Farm, with its thatched roof and "martin-haunted eaves", may be taken as a type of those picturesque abodes, whose simple rusticity strikes the traveller, when he contrasts it with the shoddiness of the more pretentious villas which mar the landscape of other parts of the parish, making him wish for older times – when man knew how to build.

Opposite the farm, set into a stone wall fronting Locksley Hall (named after an early poem by Tennyson) stood the post box from which the poet used to send poems and letters to the mainland. Locksley Hall , alas, is no longer there, but the post box with its fine VR plate, was saved, and is now in the care of the Parish Council.

Directly opposite the main entrance to Farringford in **Bedbury Lane,** is Farringford Lodge, an ornate cottage, once the home of Mr Walters, Tennyson's butler. Alongside runs a footpath known as **Granny's Mead,** which leads across the fields to **Pound Green.** Joy Lester, author of *Freshwater in Old Picture Postcards* (1983) speculates that this took its name from Granny Groves, who lived on the Farringford estate until well into her 90s, and who inspired Tennyson's poem *The Grandmother.* Also pensioned off somewhere on the Estate, where he dined on *hard-boiled eggs, cooked fifty at a time, and on dried goat's flesh,* was William Knight, a coachman who started work shortly before the arrival of the Tennysons, and who survived into his 80s, outlasting the Great War. Alfred's grandson Lionel reported that *of all human beings he was scornful and contemptuous, but he considered all Tennysons the noblest and wisest people on earth.*

Further down Bedbury Lane towards the Bay is Roseberry Lodge. James Rodgers, a friend of Tennyson and a noted explorer and naturalist, moved here in 1845. His descendant, local artist Muriel Owen, still owns two rare Cameron portraits of her great-great grandfather. Accompanied by his son Henry St John Rodgers, James made several trips to the Brazilian jungle to collect specimens, particularly butterflies. These were on behalf of Lord Rosebury, hence the (misspelt) name of the cottage. On one of these expeditions, Henry was bitten by a snake, the bite eventually proving fatal.

On the crossroads where **Bedbury Lane, Gate Lane** and **Victoria Road** meet stands Orchard's, the general store where the Tennysons shopped. First built in 1845 as a private dwelling, it was opened as a store by Mr Orchard in 1865 as can still be seen painted proudly above the front door. Its special architectural appeal lies in the fact that the latest style of patterned brick used in its construction has remained virtually unaltered to the present day. To the left was the bakehouse and to the right the original Post Office: the store itself sold food, oil, wines and spirits. On one memorable occasion both Tennyson and the American poet Henry Wadsworth Longfellow, of *Hiawatha* fame, were both seen buying pipe tobacco at the same time.

Whitecliff House in **Victoria Road** was home to Alice Liddell who stayed here with her family and was photographed by Julia Cameron as *Pomona, St Agnes* and *Alethia.* She was the little girl who served Lewis Carroll as a model for Alice in *Alice's Adventures in Wonderland* (1865). Her father (1811-1898) was successively headmaster of Westminster School and Dean of Christ Church, Oxford. The family was very much part of the Freshwater circle: Hester Fuller records that *Mrs Cameron also photographed*

Whitecliffe House in **Victoria Road, Freshwater Bay**

Alice in Wonderland, who came with her sisters and her father . . . to stay in Freshwater one summer.

The painter Augustus John (1878-1961) stayed at Monksfield during the early part of the 20th century with the Slade family at whose School in London he trained. His autobiography *Chiaroscuro* (1952) abounds with many anecdotes about writers whom he met or knew as friends.

William Allingham (1824-1889) lodged at Myrtle Cottage. His memories are captured in his *Diary* published posthumously in 1907 and provide brief, intense snapshots of Freshwater life. He adopts a kind of literary shorthand: breathless, abrupt and full of sharp detail.

> *1868. October 15th To Freshwater. Miss Thackeray at St John's Cottage with Marjorie and Annie and maid Justine. Guests – Frederick Walker, the artist, small, compact, jockeylike figure, large bluish eyes, short but thick brown hair combed down over his forehead; his small hand gives you a sinewy grip.*

An Irishman and a poet, Allingham counted Tennyson, Carlyle, Rosetti and Millais among his friends. His lifelong friendship with Tennyson began in 1851 and the poet is a central figure in his *Diary*.

Myrtle Cottage, Freshwater Bay — William Allington stayed here in 1868. An Irishman and a poet Allington counted Tennyson, Carlyle, Rosetti and Millais among his friends.

1863 October 3rd I am invited to go to the Tennysons tonight (Hurrah!) Drawing room tea, Mrs Tennyson in white, I can sometimes scarcely hear her low tones. Mrs Cameron, dark, short, sharp-eyed, one hears very distinctly . . .

1863 October 4th T. takes me upstairs to his 'den' on the top-storey, and higher, up a ladder, to the leads. He often comes up here a-night to look at the Heavens. One night he was watching shooting-stars and tumbled through the hatchway, falling on the floor below, a height of at least ten feet, I should say. The ladder probably broke his fall, and he was not hurt.

Allingham's *Diary* records a wealth of contemporary anecdote told with the wit and bonhomie of a born raconteur, interspersed with almost lyrical descriptions of the countryside. The full text is currently available both as a sumptuous Folio Society edition, with photographs by Mrs Cameron, and in the Penguin Books Lives & Letters Series. Both are introduced by John Julius Norwich who, unlike an earlier editor, the poet Geoffrey Grigson – who thought Allingham a bore whose presence was endured rather than enjoyed by Tennyson – finds the man amusing, well read and lacking in pomposity.

Allingham became a Customs officer at Lymington in Hampshire, having spent some seven gloomy years working in a bank . . . The proximity of the town made it easy for him to frequently visit Farringford. Mrs Clough, widow of the poet Arthur Hugh Clough (1819-1861) also stayed at Myrtle Cottage and knew Allingham well, accompanying him on occasion to Farringford. Julia Cameron recalled Clough's final visit to Freshwater Bay (he died in Florence) in a poem.

But eighteen months ago – and here he stood
Warm as the summer air in fullest June
Pouring all learning like a golden flood.
Now – all is vanished – too soon – too soon.

Allingham's first volume, *Poems,* was published in 1850, and contains his best known work *The Fairies (Up the airy mountain).* Several others followed, including the long work *Laurence Bloomfield in Ireland* (1864) as well as a number of collections and verse for children. Some of these were illustrated by Rosetti, Millais, Kate Greenaway, and his wife, Helen Paterson whom he married in 1874. William Allingham died in Hampstead in 1889.

Julia captures perfectly Clough's religious doubts and tragic nature, *the tender questionings of a wild unrest/of noble soul,* which make his work appear too modern and unadorned, un-Victorian even.

Opposite Freshwater Bay Post Office in **Gate Lane** is a thatched church built from ancient stone supposedly taken from a ruined cottage on nearby Hooke Hill. Local rumour has it that it was the birthplace of the scientist Robert Hooke (1635-1703) and the carved date 1694, now incorporated into the vestry wall, supposedly comes from this

Freshwater Bay Post Office — part of this building was once a local bookshop run by two spinster cousins who moved to Freshwater in 1929.

original building. In fact, the church was completed in 1909, to replace Mrs Cameron's gift of an 'Iron Room' in **The Square,** now too small for the local congregation.

Hallam Tennyson, the poet's son, donated the land on which it stands from the family estate. His (first) wife suggested the church be dedicated to St Agnes, and gave the porch in memory of her mother. The foundation stone was laid by Harold Tennyson in 1908. Inside there is a brass memorial to Anne Thackeray, under her married name of Lady Ritchie. A hundred yards or so from the church, opposite Orchard's is the start of what used to be known as Farringford Lane (or Green Lane), the original main drive to the big house, which runs up to the green door and the rustic bridge. Gerard Manley Hopkins walked these lanes, as did the Russian novelist Ivan Sergevich Turgenieff. Although neither encountered Alfred, the latter was eventually to meet him at Aldworth, in Surrey.

Next to St Agnes is Baker's Farm, an 18th century listed building. Behind the farmhouse are the remains of ancient barns. Julia Cameron travelled with the Baker family to Ceylon in 1875. Opposite is The Mall, a parade of shops built to service the needs of the new Victorian residents of Freshwater. It included an apothecary and a Mr Gubbins, official piano tuner to Queen Victoria. He also ran a library agency, and hired out baby carriages from his forecourt. This shop became, in turn, 'Woolf and Geer', local booksellers and newsagents, established by two spinster cousins who moved to Freshwater in 1929. Miss Geer became a close friend of later generations of Tennysons and was a fund of local knowledge. Part of this shop is now Freshwater Bay Post Office.

The Square is on the left, almost opposite Dimbola and **Terrace Lane.** Unfortunately The Porch, a house built by Julia Cameron, was destroyed by a German bomb during the Second World War. Two modern semis now mark the spot where it stood. Joan Brading Grayer recalls seeing the two ladies who lived there at the time being dragged lifeless from the ruins, and how *some of the debris had fallen on Dimbola, including a five-foot long beam, which embedded itself on top of the tower like a crooked flagpole.*

In 1907, Ann Thackeray took a lease on The Porch, and after the death of her husband in 1912, spent most of her time there. From her *Journal* . . .

> *This is the gate of Heaven. There is a sense of repose that I think one must feel after death before beginning the new life. (It is inconceivable how I enjoy it. I do nothing for hours together). The sitting room opens into a tiny conservatory, and through an opened window one hears the enchanted moan of the sea. I go to sleep with the sea in my ears and a star looking in at my window.*

Mrs Cameron had originally built The Porch for the use of Benjamin Jowett (1817-1893) Master of Balliol, who was then working on his edition of Plato (1871). Its name, however, derives from the ideals underlying Athenian intellectual society, the arts and sciences as one, to which the Freshwater circle aspired. Ironically, Plato banned poets from his ideal Republic.

Anne and Minnie Thackeray were brought directly to Dimbola by the Tennysons following the death of their father, the author of *Vanity Fair,* William Makepeace Thackeray, in 1863. They looked out one night to see Alfred standing outside their front window, a silent but perhaps unsettling mark of respect. In her *Journal,* Anne wrote

This sad year began at Freshwater. It was bitter weather. Minny and I were at Mrs Cameron's cottage. She was goodness in person. Alfred Tennyson used to come and see us in his cloak.

Anne Thackeray, in the words of Laura Troubridge who as a child was photographed by Julia Cameron,

> *inherited much of her father's talent as a writer, and even a sweet, pale reflection of his genius. Certainly her writings are intensely individual. She describes things as a person might name the objects flying past in a train, and they have the same effect as a chanting, dreamy monotone, enlivened by snatches of mirth and brightened by gleams of colour. One is conscious that at the back of this sweet lullaby of life there is a certain shrewd observation, a gleam of mockery . . .*
>
> Laura Troubridge: Memories and Reflections (1925)

Troubridge remembers her friend as disconnected, sweet, wholly delightful, while her eyes missed nothing. She was utterly oblivious to fashion, a sin in the eyes of Mrs Prinsep, and not unlike the White Queen in *Alice in Wonderland. From An Island* (1880) by Anne Thackeray, a novella in which Tennyson, Watts and Julia Cameron all come thinly disguised, is a comedy of manners shot through with visionary insights.

> *The firebrand in the still rippled sea turned from flame to silver as the light changed and ebbed. The light on the sea seemed dimmer, but then the land caught fire in turn, and trees and downs and distant roof-tops blazed in this great illumination, and the shadows fell black upon the turf.*

Mrs Ritchie's last book, *From The Porch* (1913), contains a rare photograph of her seaside home as well as personal reminiscences. *Records of Tennyson, Ruskin and Browning* (1892) recalls memories of an Island spring. It is like a Helen Allingham watercolour in words, with sentences that flow on seemingly forever.

> *The woods are full of anemones and primroses; narcissus grows wild in the lower fields a lovely creamy stream of flowers flows along the lanes, and lies hidden in the levels; hyacinth pools of blue shine in the woods; and then with a later burst of glory comes the gorse, lighting up the country round about, and blazing round about the beacon hill*

It was at The Porch that Lady Ritchie died, in 1919. The obituary in *The Times Literary Supplement* spoke of a writer of genius, a true artist comparable to George Eliot. It had been written by Virginia Woolf, who had stayed with Anne while recovering from one of a series of nervous breakdowns which were ultimately to lead to her drowning herself in the River Ouse in 1941. Doubtless it was at The Porch that the seeds for her play *Freshwater,* written in the early 1920s, were first sown from Anne's memories. As Virginia wrote in *Reminiscences,* her father had earlier brought her to Freshwater Bay after the death of her mother Julia in 1895 (Mrs Cameron's 'favourite niece'). On a clifftop walk, he would *show us for a moment an inspiring vision of free life, bathed in an impersonal light. There were numbers of things to learn, books to be read, and success and happiness were to be attained there without disloyalty.*

The Porch acted as Bloomsbury-on-Sea during times of crisis. The critic Desmond MacCarthy and his wife Molly, whose autobiography *A Nineteenth Century Childhood* (1924) was a particular favourite of John Betjeman, spent most of 1915 at The Porch. Molly was a niece of Anne Thackeray. Desmond was expected to write his great novel during this stay, a task at which he did not succeed. The art critic and painter Roger Fry (1866-1934) stayed nearby, with his daughter, and on one occasion the two families went together to nearby Alum Bay, where to their amusement, the rocks resembled those of the Omega workshops. Roger Fry returned later with Goldie Lowes Dickinson (1862-1932), the writer and political theorist, causing Molly to predict

> *we shall have lots of jolly, vague transcendental talk from the PostImpQuaker Swedenborgiomaterialist (ie Roger) and the Spiritualtruthfulaurasearching sodom combatting racked and tortured Goldie.*

Hugh and Mirabel Cecil: Clever Hearts (1990)

Dimbola Lodge in **Terrace Lane** was once the home of writer and pioneer photographer, Julia Margaret Cameron. Born in Calcutta in 1815, she first visited Freshwater in 1855, and in a letter already refers to *my dear Isle of Wight.* In 1860, she bought two adjacent cottages and joined them together with a Gothic tower naming the resulting house after the family tea plantations in Ceylon.

Anne Thackeray described the shock of first meeting Julia, *A strange apparition in a flowing red velvet dress, although it was summer time, cordially welcoming us to some belated meal, when the attendant butler was addressed by her as 'man' and was*

Dimbola Lodge in **Terrace Lane, Freshwater Bay** and the home of pioneer photographer Julia Margaret Cameron.

ordered to bring back the luncheon dishes and curries for which Mrs Cameron had a speciality. When we left, she came with us bareheaded and trailing draperies.

The West Wight landscape was an additional attraction and as Julia wrote in a letter in 1865

> *The elms make a golden girdle around us now. The dark purple hills of England behind are a glorious picture in the morning when the sun shines on them and the elm trees . . . there is something so wholesome in beauty, and it is not for me to try to tell of all we have here in those delicate tints of a distant bay and the still more distant headlands. These I see every day with mine own eyes.*

And yet the chance gift of a camera in 1863 led to her photographing not landscape but human figures. She followed the painter G F Watts in her attempts both at creating moral allegories and at putting together a picture gallery of famous contemporaries. Here were the great and the good, *famous men and fair maidens.* Julia Cameron's images, warts and all, have given posterity the likenesses of Tennyson (one of whose images he himself nicknamed 'the Dirty Monk'), Thomas Carlyle, Robert Browning, Charles Darwin, Henry Taylor, G F Watts and his child bride Ellen Terry, the astronomer Sir John Herschel, Richard Burton, Francis Turner Palgrave and Holman Hunt: the list is almost endless. Virtually all these photographs were taken in a reclaimed chicken house!

> *A glazed fowl house that I had given to my children became my glass house. The society of hens and chickens was soon changed for that of poets, prophets, painters and lovely maidens, who all in turn have immortalised this little farm erection.*
>
> Julia Margaret Cameron: Annals of My Glass House (written 1874, published 1927)

With less artistic success, Julia also stage-managed, and then photographed, tableaux from the Bible, Shakespeare, Greek mythology, and the works of Tennyson, an illustrated edition of whose *Idylls of the King* was her final project before leaving finally for Ceylon in 1875. Here she died four years later. Her final word, as she looked out from her mountain-top balcony at the starry night sky, was reportedly *beautiful,* a fitting epitaph for the quality she most searched for in her art.

Her husband, Charles Hay Cameron, wrote some unpublished couplets, quoted by Agnes Weld, about their new home in Freshwater.

> *There dwell I, fronting Afton Down*
> *With little Yarmouth for my nearest town . . .*
> *And hear the Nightingale that sings unseen*
> *In the dark ilex, on the flowr'y green*
> *That carpets Farringford's muse-haunted scene*

That most magical of songbirds unites the Cameron's home with that of Tennyson, just up the road and clearly audible from Dimbola. Julia herself translated the German verse romance Leonora, and wrote some fine sonnets, including her own epitaph as a photographer, *On A Portrait,* first published in September 1875.

Charles Darwin, the great naturalist came to **Redoubt House** in **Terrace Lane, Freshwater Bay** in the summer of 1869 . . . *yellow, sickly and very quiet.*

Genius and love have each fulfilled their part, and both unite with force and equal grace, whilst all we love best in classic art is stamped forever on the human face.

The breathlessness of Julia's verbal flow can be seen in the length of her sentences: her letters continue from the bottom of the page to flow up and down the margins. It is the same kind of innate generosity – which Emily Tennyson's *Journal* mildly tut- tuts about – which led to Henry Taylor writing that *Dimbola was a house indeed to which everyone resorted for pleasure, and in which no man, woman or child, was ever known to be unwelcome.* Or to remain unphotographed! As Hester Fuller recalls, *When a friend remonstrated that the passers-by were picking her sweet briar and that there would soon be none left, she answered, "but that is why I planted it so that it should be picked and enjoyed".*

Dimbola has been saved from threatened demolition by the formation of a charitable trust and the sweet briar hedge replanted. The house again echoes to the sound of music and poetry, as well as the clatter of china from the restored dining room.

In a letter, Julia Cameron recalls that same room. *Then we have feasts of intellect. We dined at 7.00pm and only got up from dinner at 11.00pm. All this while the most brilliant conversation took place. Each one recited favourite passages from Beaumont and Fletcher, favourite sonnets of Shakespeare's. Alfred and Mr Cameron were like two brilliant fencers crossing their rapiers, or flashing their foils giving and evading clean thrusts.*

Now a team of volunteers is busily restoring Dimbola to its former pristine state and the wheel has come full circle.

Dimbola is not the only house of note in **Terrace Lane.** Charles Darwin (1809-1882), the great naturalist came to Redoubt House in precarious health in the summer of 1869. William Allingham describes him as *yellow, sickly, very quiet.* Darwin's daughter, however, records that *it was a beautiful summer and we had a very entertaining time.*

Alfred Tennyson, who had prefigured some of the ideas later set out in *The Origin of Species* (1859) in *In Memoriam* (1850), was reassured to find Charles Darwin *very kindly, unworldly and agreeable. A said to him "Your theory of Evolution does not make against Christianity" and Darwin answered, "No, certainly not".*

Darwin was caught by Mrs Cameron, and thrust in front of her camera. He said of the resulting portrait that *I like this photograph very much better than any other which has been taken of me,* this despite looking extremely close to the great apes from which he thought Humankind descended. He later wrote to Julia to say, *there are sixteen people in my house, and every one is your friend.* Hester Thackeray Fuller recalls that

> *Darwin brought his horse with him. Darwin's daughter told me how her father rode up to Afton Down the first morning and let the reins drop to see what his steed would do. The horse paused for a moment and then went straight off in the direction of Darwin's home, from whence they had come.*

Redoubt House also played host to Jenny Lind 'the Swedish nightingale', that most famous of prima donnas. Emily Tennyson records in her *Journal* that Madame Goldschmidt dines at Farringford and sings two special requests of the poet, *Auld Lang*

Pannells, built next door to Redoubt House in **Terrace Lane, Freshwater Bay** was home to Tennyson's brother Frederick. Another resident was the poet Phillip Stanhope Worsley.

35

Syne and *Auld Robin Gray,* as well as some Handel and two Swedish songs, which set her voice off wonderfully. When Jenny Lind was practising her scales at Redoubt House, her voice was so penetrating that it could be heard by fishermen in the bay!

Pannells, built next door to Redoubt House, was originally called St Catherine's House. After her mother's death, Hester Thackeray Fuller sold both her Chelsea home and The Porch to buy Pannells, and from there edited Anne Thackeray's *Letters* (1924), as well as co-writing her biography, *Thackeray's Daughter* (1951) with Violet Hammersley. Hester also revisited the past in *Three Freshwater Friends.*

> *The house next to Redoubt was built for Tennyson's brother Frederick. Many interesting people have stayed there. Dean Bradley, the famous Dean of Westminster, Leslie Stephen, his sister the mystic . . . The house was christened Pannells by Hallam, Lord Tennyson. In the old charters of the Farringford estate as far back as the 12th century, 'pannells' means a small patch of ground.*

An earlier resident was the poet Philip Stanhope Worsley, who produced what Matthew Arnold considered some of the best translations of Homer, and who died young of consumption, despite Mrs Cameron's devoted nursing.

Terrace House was Tennyson's Dower House and it originally belonged to a local seaman and entrepreneur (i.e. smuggler) Jacob Long who sold the two cottages to Julia Cameron. The poet bought the property from her primarily to keep it undeveloped, and his views from Farringford unobstructed. Later he leased it to his brother Horatio, whose name appears on the 1871 Gazetteer for Freshwater as resident there.

Agnes Weld wrote of him, that *never was a man better fitted to make an ideal parish priest, yet he never could be persuaded to think himself worthy of becoming a clergyman, and so his magnificent voice was only heard in lay ministry at the bedsides of the sick and the dying to whom he would insist on carrying off any special dainty intended for his own dinner – a meal which he would constantly omit to come home to – his hunger forgotten.*

Hester Fuller writes of the house, with its handsome iron gates, as interesting for its beautiful views of the English Channel, and the remembrance that Benjamin Jowett (1817-1893) of Oxford fame *came here Spring after Spring to be near his friend the Poet.* It is certainly more commodious than The Porch ever was.

West of Freshwater Bay lies Watcombe Bay and on the approach to what is now Tennyson Down is a niche in the cliff face which Hallam declared was one of his father's favourite resting places, one *where he would often sit, sheltered from the cold winds, gazing seawards.* Agnes Weld recalls how, at this same spot,

> *my uncle stopped to point out the sunlight gilding to a deeper golden shade the fragile rockcistus bloom at his feet, and tenderly plucking the delicate flower, he held it lovingly, and said, "There is not a flower on all this Down that owes to the sun what I owe to Christ".*

Elsewhere, Tennyson sternly forbade the picking of wild flowers on his property. It was to Watcombe Bay that Tennyson walked with a young lady he had rescued from Mrs Cameron's photographic studio. He gave her his hand to help her down the steep path into Watcombe Bay, of which he was extremely proud, and showed her all the wealth of minute animal life that fills its limpid rock-pools.

Freshwater Bay — the building in the centre of the picture is The Albion and behind it Plumley's Hotel, where Tennyson stayed while viewing Farringford

Plumley's Hotel — When the artist George Morland stayed there in 1799, it was called the George Inn.

Fort Redoubt was built in the 1860s to defend the Bay from French attack. The children of its Master Gunner, Thomas Keown, provided photographic models for Mrs Cameron. Anne Thackeray wrote, *these were the children who used to come down from the fort with flowers and who planted Mrs Cameron's banks with primrose roots.* For many years a tea-room, the fort is now a private residence.

Freshwater Bay itself is dominated by an imposing white structure approached by **Gate Lane.** Freshwater Bay House, formerly known as Plumley's Hotel, has a long and fascinating history. When the artist George Morland (1763-1804), who also lived for a time at Easton Cottage, stayed there in 1799, it was called The George Inn and the Landlord was a Mr Plumley.

Impecunious as most of us are who earn their living by the brush or pen, Morland was hiding from his creditors. He painted inn signs and local subjects, including Mr Plumley in the uniform of the Isle of Wight Volunteers. On one occasion a sketching trip to Yarmouth brought disaster. *One fine drawing in particular, though it was only a spaniel dog in a landscape, was construed by the honest lieutenant of the militia into the plan of the Island, and the dog, he was confident, represented the very part of it upon which the enemy were to land.* To make matters worse, Morland had been staying at the home of wealthy smuggler George Cole. He was arrested without further ado by nine soldiers before breakfast and marched in chains to Newport jail!

Tennyson stayed at Plumley's Hotel while viewing Farringford, and later guests included Lewis Carroll and Anthony Trollope, author of the Barchester novels. Plumley's attracted the rich and the famous, the 'poshocrats' who drew Isherwood and Auden's disdain while they were in more humble lodgings. The hotel was later known as Lambert's: directly beneath it was a 'Marine Bathing House', whose foundations still survive. Under new owners, HF Holidays, the author and Oxford don J I M Stewart would come to spend the summer, to write detective novels, under his pen name Michael Innes.

Immediately opposite The Albion is Beach House, now divided into apartments and renamed Afton Down House. William Allingham wrote in a letter that *it is interesting to hear of John Milton's descendants in Beach House, especially as my friend Mrs Tennant and her daughters, living under the same roof, are the lineal descendants of Oliver Cromwell.* Regicides both!

J M W Turner stayed at The Albion in 1795 while on a youthful sketching trip. His Isle of Wight sketchbook, in pencil and watercolour, still survives and one rough sketch provided the template for his first completed oil painting, 'Fishermen at Sea', exhibited the following year and now housed in the Tate Gallery in London. It is an unsettling view of boats on a stormy sea, lit by moonlight and their own small lanterns, while the Needles loom in the background. *The Critical Guide* spotted his talent early, *the boats are buoyant and swim well, and the undulation of the element is admirably deceiving.* Not for the easily seasick.

The Albion was another favourite drinking venue of George Morland when it was a small inn (the present childrens' room) called The Cabin. Here he consorted with the smugglers, fishermen and poachers who became the subjects of his art. As Morland himself said, *where could I find such a picture of life as that (exhibiting his sketchbook) unless among the originals of The Cabin.*

Morland also frequented another nearby hostelry, The Mermaid. As Plumleys became more grand, The Albion retained its raffish atmosphere. By Mrs Cameron's time, it had become known as The Royal Albion, and was much used by the soldiers from Fort Redoubt. Christopher Isherwood, who stayed in the 1920s, recalled a *biscuit-coloured building with small classical pillars, permanently shabby because the salt spray ruined each fresh coat of paint within a week.*

Isherwood also captures the strangely intimate setting of the place *The Bay lay wedged between two immense masses of cliffs; it was so tiny you were like an actor on the stage of a theatre – anybody at any of the windows in the little semicircle of boarding houses could follow your every movement.* It is a characteristic it retains today. The Bay has long attracted painters: Turner, Morland, John Martin, John Nixon, Augustus John, G F Watts and the French impressionist Berthe Moriot. Its visual splendour – a calm haven in a stormy sea – provides the setting for Tennyson's *Enoch Arden* (1864):

> *Long lines of cliff breaking have left a chasm;*
> *And in the chasm are foam and yellow sands;*
> *Beyond red roofs about a narrow wharf.*

Like the Victorian Age in all its pomp and glory, these sands have ebbed somewhat, and roofs expanded, in the intervening years! Tennyson considered that in the later line *the league long roller thundering on the reef,* he had captured the sound of the sea. Of the same Bay, John Tyndall (1820-1893), Professor of Natural History at the Royal Institution in 1853, wrote, *I sat near the shore, observing the advance of the waves and listening to their thunder. The collisions of the flint pebbles are innumerable. They blend together in a continuous sound which could not be better described than by the*

No fewer than three literary giants have lodged at **Ocean View** in **Coastguard Lane, Freshwater Bay.** George Bernard Shaw in 1889, and Christopher Isherwood and W H Auden in 1926.

line in 'Maud' (much criticised by reviewers) "Now to the scream of a madden'd beach drag'd down by the wave".

Emily Tennyson's *Journal* records the terrifying results when humans are pitted against such natural violence, watched impotently by those on shore.

> *A fearful storm and shipwreck. The tarbarrel & lights are seen to burn a few minutes or a quarter of hour as some say and wild cries are heard or fancied & then all is silent and dark. A board floats in with 'The Hope' on it. Every soul on board has perished within sight of many on shore*

Hester Fuller adds a gentler view of the Bay, and its effect on Tennyson.

> *In 'Geraint and Enid', I always think that the dress which Earl Doorm offered Enid is like our sea at Freshwater on a calm summer day, 'Where, like a shoaling sea, the lovely blue, play'd into green.*

No wonder that Mrs Cameron brought Tennyson down here – in costume, no less – as Neptune (would that a photograph survived!), and married him to the waves.

If Tennyson was the most famous of Victorian poets in his time, then Gerard Manley Hopkins (1844-1889) was perhaps the least known. It was only posthumously that his meticulous attention to detail – seemingly so modern – reached a wider audience. If Alfred's every movement was remarked by observers, Hopkins came to Freshwater Bay in 1863, unnoticed.

Hopkins' eyes and ears were equally as acute as the Laureate's, though. Watching waves breaking on shingle becomes a scientific task; verbs have an energy and sharpness which look back to Anglo-Saxon verse, yet at the same time, forward to the late Ted Hughes (1918- 1998)

> *The shores are swimming and the eyes have before them a region of milky surf; but it is hard for them to unpack the huddling and gnarling of the water . . . the shapes and sequences of the running; I catch, however, the looped or forked wisp made by every big pebble the backwater runs over . . . then I see it run browner, the foam dwindling and twitched into long chains of suds, while the strength of the back-draught shrugged the stones together and clocked them one against another.*

W H Gardner: Gerard Manley Hopkins 2nd Edition (1948)

The very opposite of a pedant, D H Lawrence (1885-1930) stayed at Freshwater Bay in August 1909, and three years later published his novel *The Trespasser.* Based upon a true story provided him by Helen Corke, it is the tale of a young woman who escapes with her music teacher for five days – and nights – to the Isle of Wight. He returns to his wife and children and later kills himself. The finest passages of the novel are those set in Freshwater and Totland, picturing a dream-like summer with swooning intensity.

> *Siegmund had found a white cave welling with green water brilliant and full of life as mounting sap. The white rock glimmered through the water, and soon Siegmund shimmered also in the living green of the sea, like pale flowers trembling upwards.*

He swims from this cave – beneath Fort Redoubt – into Watcombe Bay: the topography is still clear, even if Lawrence does not provide any names. In this charged world, everything is sexual.

> *Throwing himself down on sand that was soft and warm as white fur, he lay glistening wet, panting, swelling with glad pride at having conquered also this small, inaccessible sea-cave, creeping into it like a white bee into a white virgin blossom.*

Saucy postcards on sale in local shops seem to tap into an equally primeval seam, the association of the sea not just with death but sex, love and romance. Even the notoriously reined-in T S Eliot came to Freshwater Bay in the 1950s, for three weeks with his sister in 1954, and then with her and his second wife, Valerie, in 1957. Fifty years earlier, Rudyard Kipling rented a house with the American writer Wolcott Balestier and his sister. In 1920, Kipling and Carole Balestier, now his wife, returned for a nostalgic visit.

No less than three literary giants have lodged at Ocean View in **Coastguard Lane.** George Bernard Shaw spent his honeymoon there in 1898, while novelist Christopher Isherwood and poet W H Auden lodged there in 1926. Shaw passed the time writing *Caesar and Cleopatra* on Tennyson Down while Isherwood and Auden sang hymns every evening to the latter's fierce piano accompaniment. Christopher Isherwood recalls the decor at Ocean View, run by chain-smoking Miss Chichester, with a kind of amused horror.

> *Nothing had been moved. The frosted glass lamp still stood in the middle of the table cloth with its woollen pom-poms. The Maiden's Prayer still hung over the fireplace, and above the piano was the photograph of Lord Tennyson, described by the poet as the 'Dirty Monk'. How happy I felt in this room.*
>
> Christopher Isherwood: Lions and Shadows: An Education in the Twenties (1938)

One wonders if this picture was a Cameron original. In his poem *August for the people and their favourite islands,* written for Isherwood on his birthday, Auden commemorates those times, nine years before on that southern island, *when half-boys, we spoke of books and praised/the acid and austere.* It was dreamtime, soon to be ended:

> *Scented our turf, the distant baying*
> *Nice decoration to the artist's wish;*
> *Yet fast the deer was flying through the wood*

Isherwood returned alone the following year, and worked on his novel *All the Conspirators* (1928), which drew on his experiences of that first Island visit, as did the later *Lions and Shadows.* It is that work which now reads more excitingly, as with a meticulousness later copied by Mass Observation, Isherwood captures the petty rituals and staidness of the English middle class male, from which his own covert homosexuality (later explored in his 1976 book, *Christopher and his Kind)* distanced him.

> *What was it that made them perform their grave ritual of pleasure; putting on blazers and flannels in the morning, plus-fours or white trousers in the afternoon, dinner jackets in the evening; playing tennis, golf, bridge; dancing, without a smile, the fox-trot, the tango, the blues;*

smoking their pipes, reading the newspapers, a sing song, distributing prizes after a fancy-dress ball.

It is a world from which Isherwood is in full flight: henceforth he would be a camera. *The most I shall ever achieve will be to learn how to spy upon them, unnoticed. Henceforth, my problem is how to perfect a disguise.* Next stop, Berlin.

In 1928, Isherwood was joined by his friend and fellow novelist Edward Falaise Upward, born in Essex in 1903 but raised in Sandown and a lifelong friend, whose novel, *In The Thirties* (1962) begins with an account of this holiday and his own abandonment of writing poetry. Isherwood and Upward were at Repton and Corpus Christi College, Cambridge together, and collaborated in writing some of their surreal imaginary world of 'Mortmere' while on the Island. An open air dance held outside The Albion, with music from a down-at-heel brass band made Alan feel that he was seeing the human race as it really was, sublime, infinitely finer than all the gods and goddesses it had ever invented. The Marxist Upward sees behind this happiness, through the inevitable rot which will come upon them and the historic tragedy of women.

Little wonder then, that the hero of In The Thirties at one point contemplates suicide, and walks up to Afton Down to throw himself off the cliff.

> *The bland, sunny sea, unwrinkled from the horizon inwards towards the very beach below the cliff, looking as if it had never drowned anyone . . . as he stood watching from so near the cliff-edge, he became convinced that fear had not been the only cause of his failure to throw himself over. He had been deterred also by the desire – and the sea had made him aware of it – to go on living.*
>
> Edward Upward: In The Thirties (1962)

In The Thirties is the first novel of a magnificent trilogy. *The Spiral Ascent* (completed in 1977) traces this life, a politically engaged one (Upward was for some years a member of the Communist Party), through to CND and opposition to the Vietnam War.

Upward's story *At the Ferry Inn* recounts a later meeting with a friend, now a famous writer exiled in New York, whom one presumes is Isherwood. The two violently disagree – about Auden's political commitment, of all things – and the last he sees of his former colleague is on the ferry back to the mainland. Not drowning but waving.

W H Auden once wrote a poem commissioned to accompany a film about the Island. Though never used as such, it provided the basis for his poem, *Look, stranger, on this island now.*

> *Here at the small field's ending pause*
> *When the chalk wall falls to the foam and its tall ledges*
> *Oppose the pluck*
> *And knock of the tide,*
> *And the shingle scrambles after the sucking surf,*
> *And the gull lodges*
> *A moment on its sheer side*

Freshwater Bay's very name suggests a place of beneficence and healing. It was here that weary sailors could put in for fresh supplies, sweetness rather than salt. Behind the sea wall, Sandpipers' Hotel – founded by a Temperance pioneer – now plays host to a craft shop stocking only locally-made products. The popular writer Cassandra Eason lives

Glenbrook St Francis, Freshwater Bay — now the Promenade Holiday Flats,was once the dower house of Lady May Tennyson, Hallam's second wife. As May Prinsep she had been frequently photographed by Julia Cameron.

nearby, author of new age manuals like *The Psychic Power of Children,* books which empower.

As the pre-Raphaelite artist Holman Hunt – who painted *The Light of the World,* and also Tennyson – wrote in thanks to Emily after a short stay in the Bay, *my holiday brought me balm and health and I went back to my work with renewed zest.*

The coast road, **Military Road,** climbs steeply up from the Bay towards **Ventnor** passing as it does Promenade Holiday Flats, which were previously known as Glenbrook St Francis, the Dower House of Lady May Tennyson, Hallam's second wife. As May Prinsep, she had been much photographed by Julia Cameron. She played an active part in local community life and

> *raised money for the West Wight Ambulance and planned a lending library. To this end Lady Tennyson bought the rather ugly house at the foot of Afton Down beside old Mr Cotton's boat house (now the Inshore Rescue Building). Every morning she set off in a fly to pick up Hester Thackeray and spend the day with her sorting books and eating bananas like school girls! They were helped in their task by Lady Tennyson's librarian, Allan May.*
>
> Belinda Thackeray Norman-Butler: Three Freshwater Friends (3rd Edition 1992)

During the Great War, Lady May also supervised the Afton Red Cross Hospital, where some 1500 patients had been admitted. The ambulance service – maintained by a volunteer crew – is still active, its vehicle instantly recognisable by its number plate,

VDL 1. Dispersed volumes from the St Francis library – with Lady May's signature on the flyleaf – still turn up in local secondhand bookshops.

Allan May was also a local poet of note, with a weekly verse published in the Isle of Wight County Press, and work read on the BBC. *Thoughts and Dreams of Quiet Hours* (1926) now seems less interesting than the fact that its author was a Franciscan lay reader who dressed like a monk, was supposedly a hermaphrodite and spoke in a fine though somewhat sibilant voice.

Eric Ratcliffe's *The Golden Heart Man* (1993) collects anecdotes and selects poems, while May's position of local literary eccentric is now filled by Bruce Laker – who got married in a wedding dress under his female name of Phaedra Kelly – and writes learned articles about 'transconscience' for crossdressing magazines worldwide.

The most distinguished guest at Glenbrook between the wars was Haile Selassie, the exiled Emperor of Ethiopia, who would walk with his retinue down the middle of Gate Lane, confident that no motorist would dare to harm his Imperial Majesty. The most likely reason for the Emperor's visit was his desire to retrace the steps of one of his royal predecessors, the young Prince Alamayu, who had stayed at Farringford with his guardian, Captain Speedy. Selassie was later canonised by Jamaican Rastafarians – including Bob Marley of No Woman, No Cry fame – as the Lion of Judah, the mystical leader of black Africa. He might well have been the guest of Evelyn Prinsep – a distant relative of Julia Cameron – at Glenbrook. Evelyn had commanded an Indian regiment, and married an aristocratic Russian refugee whose family had been attached to the Court. The girl's father had sent her, his only daughter, to Vladivostock to find sanctuary with the British forces there. Colonel Prinsep fell in love immediately, and they were married almost at once despite finding *she had no stockings for her wedding, and her legs were cut and bleeding from sabre slashes.* This is the Evelyn Prinsep whose *Freshwater Gates: A Miscellany* was privately published from this address at Christmas 1945, and printed on the presses of the Isle of Wight County Press.

In a bizarre series of poems, stories and articles, dealing with everything from disappearing donkeys to the works of Pushkin, tales from the Somme to verse dedicated to Lord Baden-Powell, the sentiments of the title poem at least are still relevant. It also disproves the adage that all poems need to do is rhyme.

The sheer ineptitude of the verse construction – abab, then abba – the way words are either missed out or added to conform to the iambic rhythm, and the forced rhymes ('fungus' broken across two lines in a manner that has to be unique), all almost rival William McGonagall. The poem is grandly appended with Prinsep's good wishes to the Council for the Preservation of Rural England.

> *Between the Needles and Black Gang*
> *The hand of man is rarely seen;*
> *But this is where great poet sang*
> *His 'Idylls of the King' to Queen.*
> *But where the hand of man has been*
> *Was beauty's knell by fashion rung,*
> *By bricks and mortar like a fung-*
> *Us, hideous growth on sylvan sheen.*

And yet, strangely, one knows exactly what he is getting at . . .

Chapter Two
Freshwater, Brook, Brighstone & Shorwell

At the junction of School Green and **Afton Down** roads in Freshwater is **Hooke Hill.** The scientist and architect Robert Hooke (1635-1703) was born in a cottage near All Saints Church – there is a small museum to his memory – in the road now named in his honour. There is a memorial plaque to him at the bottom of the hill, in front of the Co-op. Many of Hooke's writings changed the view of the physical world of the time. An inventor, creator of scientific laws (notably Hooke's Law which postulates the relationship between stress and strain in an elastic material when it is stretched), and a leading member of the Royal Society, Hooke predated Isaac Newton in having a complete picture of a mechanical system of the universe founded on universal gravitation. He was a pioneer in anatomy, geology and physics and Sir Christopher Wren built the dome of St Paul's Cathedral using Hooke's principle of the 'catenary curve'.

Hooke's most important scientific treatise is *Micrographia* – small things seen large – which was last reprinted in 1968. Hooke's Diaries were edited by Richard Nichols in 1994, with the subtitle *The Leonardo of London.*

Next to the Co-op, Honnor and Jeffrey's Garden Centre shares the same site as The End-of-the-Line Café which is part of the former railway station closed by Dr Beeching in 1953. Tennyson would have approved. The rapid growth of Freshwater in the late 19th century from a quiet backwater into a fashionable resort had been startling and the spread of holiday villas inspired him to write,

> *Yonder lies our young sea-village – Art and Grace are less and less, Science grows and beauty dwindles – roofs of slated hideousness.*

Shortly after Tennyson's arrival in 1853, his brother Charles Tennyson Turner records . . .

> *a few small houses and a little white hotel by the Bay, a few more houses clustered round the old church by the river, and sparsely scattered about the winding lanes of 'elm and whispering oak' old stone cottages and seventeenth century farms with roofs of thatch or stone tiling.*

By 1880, a local guidebook could write glowingly that Freshwater Bay is *a rising and fashionable watering place, the facility for bathing being extended.* White's *Directory 1859* lists mainly farmers, blacksmiths, grocers, wheelwrights and the like, along with a few inns and taverns. The only profession of note, other than 'gentleman' or 'Poet Laureate' are those of 'gunner' and 'lighthouse keeper'. Hill's *Directory 1879,* twenty years later lists a profusion of 'furnished apartments' for rent: new arrivals include insurance agents, photographers, coaching establishments, dissenting ministers and surgeons.

Even worse was the rise in the numbers of excursions from the mainland. A major factor in this early tourist boom was the coming of the railways notably the Freshwater, Yarmouth and Newport Railway which eventually opened for business in August 1889. An extension originally planned for Totland had been successfully thwarted as Emily recorded in her *Journal* for March, 1865, *the threatened railway with a terminus at the Bay is to be stopt at Hook Hill or Pound Green. Not welcome to us even then.* The FYN kept the idea alive until the late-1890s when it was eventually dropped because the tourist industry failed to attract sufficient custom. A little like today, perhaps.

The introduction of statutory Bank Holidays in 1871 meant that working people could visit the Island as day-trippers. These were the 'cockneys', whose presence so annoyed the poet, but whose purchase of mass-marketed editions of his work made him so rich. He was thus able to build a second mansion, in Aldworth – remote on a hillside on the Hampshire/Surrey border – where he could escape them.

As early as October 1864, that writer of deliberate nonsense Edward Lear sensed this gathering cloud of disillusion, though he would have enjoyed a pleasant evening *had not Mrs Cameron come in.* Lear and Tennyson walk to Alum Bay – which Alfred thought they were *just spoiling* – but Edward finds that

> *He doesn't seem to enjoy scenery now, and ever talks about the accursed railway. At dinner, AT's ravings about England going downhill. "Best thing God can do is squash the planet flat". AT's manner is assuredly odious at times. I believe no woman in all this world could live with him for a month.*

Lear, who never married, seemed half in love with Emily himself. He named his villa in San Remo after her, and described her as that *near angel woman.*

Just before **School Green Road** meets **Brookside Road** is Freshwater Library and Gallery. It was frequently used by J B Priestley when it first opened during the Second World War.In less impecunious times it proved a magnet for local arts activity, including special exhibitions by the Dorset based KQBX Press featuring their in-house artist Dave Eyre, early one-person shows by Emma Bradford and Julian Bell, and a rafter-raising poetry reading by black Mancunian Lemn Sissay.

All Saints Church is at the top of **Hooke Hill** and is one of only two Island churches to still have some Saxon masonry in evidence. In a letter written in 1859, Edward Lear calculates that

> *computing moderately that fifteen angels, several hundreds of ordinary women, many philosophers, a heap of truly kind and wise mothers, three or four minor prophets and a lot of doctors and schoolmistresses might all be boiled down, and yet their combined essence fell short of what Emily Tennyson really is.*

A similar act of homage informs Ann Thwaite's *Emily Tennyson: the Poet's Wife* (1996), a bold and scholarly attempt to prove Anne Thackeray's opinion that *she too was a poet in her life and fervent feeling, though she did not write it down.* Emily now lies buried in the churchyard here, in the Tennyson family plot. Mary Hillier, Julia Cameron's favourite model is nearby. In the south aisle is a stained glass window, designed by G F Watts, featuring a rather feminine Sir Galahad, and Emily Tennyson as an angel.

There is a touching memorial in Latin to Lionel Tennyson, the poet's son buried at sea, and a splendid head-and-shoulders sculpture of Alfred by the sculptress Mignon Jones, based on Mrs Cameron's photographs and restoring the poet's robustness. Even the church clock rings out a tune composed by Sir John Stainer in the poet's honour, and known for ever after as the 'Tennyson chimes'. The Tennyson family vault is to the east of the church and overlooks the Yar estuary.

> *An angel folds its wings, huddled warm*
> *I pass by, cosy as the couples lying ended-*
> *different dates, their joint lives ended*
> *by a stonemason's chisel. "Greatly mourned"*
>
> *The boneyard ebbs down to the sea,*
> *despite the yews, buds foretell the Spring.*
> *Flowers die in jars, from death snowdrops spring,*
> *Gulls circle back like white debris.*
>
> *I cloak in my warmth, feel its passing, but*
> *Walk towards the cold shore's culmination.*
> *The church clock ticks towards culmination.*
> *The lych gate swings sharply shut.*
>
> Brian Hinton: Island Churchyard (1983)

From the church, the **Causeway** heads west towards **Newport Road** passing Afton Manor as it does so. The Cotton family lived here in Tennyson's time, one of whose daughters was targeted as a potential wife for the eternal bachelor, Edward Lear. Emily's strategy did not succeed. From **Newport Road, Manor Road** and **Southdown Road** lead into **Military Road** and **Afton Down,** scene of a phenomenon unique in the annals of pop music, the 1970 Isle of Wight Pop Music Festival. Forced by the County Council of the time into a site not of their choosing, ironically, through either malice or bungling, the result was a natural amphitheatre, and a stage behind which the sun would set each night on the magnificence of Tennyson Down, the poet's monument a fiery beacon atop it. Glorious weather and 'good vibes' combined to create an unforgettable weekend for those who came. One of the faceless multitude of the time – Bob Geldorf – might well have got the idea for 'Live Aid' from the sense of community engendered here.

> *Three pounds, ten shillings to come inside the magic compound,*
> *Striking camp like Custer, recolonising the native ground.*
> *Stoned, drowning in music that throbs sweet in scented air*
> *so charged it can be touched. Beneath Afton Down we cast care*
> *aside with clothes, to light our fragile way to illumination;*
> *lost, weightless, we cascade down an avalanche of imagination.*
>
> Brian Hinton: Fiery Creations (1989)

Among those the crowd's imagination were Joni Mitchell's careful, crafted and coherent lyrics, Leonard Cohen – already a published poet and novelist – and Jim Morrison of The Doors (itself a name taken from William Blake). Morrison's two rare poetry collections,

The Lords (1969) and *New Creatures* (1969) continue to circulate amongst fans, as does the posthumous *Wilderness: The Lost Writings* (1988).

Festival headliner Jimi Hendrix played a version of the National Anthem, as well as some of the questing, unrealised songs planned for *First Rays of The New Rising Sun,* finally released to the public in 1997. *Recorded Poems* (1986) gathers his lyrics, which have great imaginative power, even when divorced from their musical arrangements. Within a year of the Festival, both Morrison and Hendrix were dead, strangely romantic icons who have since refused to quit the public imagination.

Elsewhere during the event packed weekend, Procol Harum chanted out the hypnotic words of their full-time poet and lyricist, Keith Reid – as obsessed with death as Edgar Allan Poe.

The Who went even further and performed the bulk of their rock opera *Tommy* written by lead guitarist Pete Townshend. Folk-singer Donovan sang some of his songs for children, proving him to be the spiritual descendant, in pure nonsense, of Edward Lear.

The film, video, CD and my book of this event, *Message to Love* (1995), all record the Festival's end, a mad mixture of bad debts, ill-feeling, crowd violence and an overarching sense of elegy for the 60s dream. This is perfectly captured in compere Ricki Farr's words of farewell to the crowd – *You've all been beautiful. Even those who tore down the fences.*

In *The Road Goes On Forever* (1982) Philip Norman (of whom much more later in Ryde) traced the future history of the three Foulk brothers – Ron, Ray and Bill – who had grown up on the Island, and masterminded all three Pop Festivals.

Where, one wonders, is Ron Smith, the genial Brummie who helped save Newport's Quay Arts Centre, and has since organised the restoration of Dimbola, but started off as the site engineer on all three events?

Stand for a moment on Afton Down as the setting sun balances precariously on the top of Tennyson's monument, and you might *just* catch the last echoes of a Hendrix riff before the night gathers all up before it and leaves just a vibrating silence behind.

The coast which stretches from Freshwater Bay round to Ventnor remains to this day, a dangerous and unforgiving place, with vicious currents, hidden rocks and no safe harbour. William Allingham records in his usual terse way a walk with Tennyson in 1867, over Afton Down to Brook Bay:

> . . . *ship ashore, the 'Fannie Larabie' of Bath, large, three masts, good model. There are people on the shore but T. doesn't seem to mind. We walked to next point and saw a steamer ashore at Atherfield, then turned up to downs and came back by a path slanting along the cliff side, like a frightful dream rather, my head being lightish.*
> *T. tells of people who have fallen over, and at one place is a monumental stone to commemorate such an accident. I said (walking close behind him) "suppose I were to slip and catch hold of you, and we both rolled down together" on which T. stopped and said, " You'd better go first".*

The memorial to an unfortunate girl who took such a one-way plunge, with its reassuring statement *in the midst of life we are in death* to cheer the casual walker, is still there.

Tennyson often sounds like an old pet dog, desperate for 'Walkies'. In October 1868, Allingham records a walk eastwards across the hills.

> *We find the Tennyson carriage at Miss Thackeray's. Mrs T. asks the ladies "Will you take compassion on him", that is allow AT to walk with them and they do consent. We walk off down old road, by Afton Park fence, field-path through turnips to Afton Down, see the barrows (ancient burial mounds) cross the rough, new Military Road, and by path to shore; geology – Wealden; so on to Brook Point and the fossil trees.*
>
> *T. (enjoying girls' company) says, "If I could take a walk like this every day I shouldn't be tired of Freshwater".*

Brook Hill House, Brook, with its unequalled views westward to Tennyson Down, was the home of
J B Priestley between 1948 and 1959

Two miles or so along Military Road and some of the Island's most spectacular natural views, is the turning which leads to **Brook.** About a mile down Brook Road, on the right, a narrow lane leads to Brook Hill House, home of J B Priestley (1894-1984) between 1948 and 1959. The house is a magnificently sumptuous Edwardian folly, with superb, unequalled views westward towards Tennyson Down – Farringford and the poet's monument are both clearly visible – and the mainland beyond. At night, the great man would challenge his guests that they could *look at the lights of Bournemouth and thank God you're not there.*

Peter Davison found a landscape of ruins, *strange swales and lanes and heights and views and winds.* The working day would start with a huge breakfast, with *hot dishes of kidneys, kippers on the sideboard at a stated hour,* after which Priestley would disappear into his study until lunchtime, to re-emerge for *fierce tennis on the private court,* tea on the terrace, cocktails, and a late and lavish dinner. Priestley's second wife, Jane, meanwhile supervised the home farm with its herd of pedigree cows, and the large estate with all its retinue of tenants and servants. Just like Alfred and Emily really, and J B Priestley in his plainer, prosier way (he had been born in Bradford, son of a schoolmaster) was just as much a template of his age, an exemplar of contemporary Englishness.

The novelist himself described the local landscape as *the scenery of our dreams,* and captures the view from his study window as if in a painting, framed and frozen in time. Priestley was a keen watercolourist. He looks down on Brook village, with its small chapel to St Mary the Virgin, and the remains of Brook Manor.

> *Down below are downlands and heath, green slopes and gorse in bloom. Lower and nearer the centre are cultivated fields, then beyond, just in the picture, a glimpse of a tiny church, and the ruin of a large manor house . . . Further off, but dominating the scene, is the long chalk cliff that ends in the Needles. And full in the middle panes of my window is that flashing mirror, that blue diamond or that infinite haze, that window for the mind, which is the sea.*

J B Priestley: Delight (1949)

Delight rings with the ardour of the newly converted. Although there is something relentlessly stagey about Priestley's work, these essays, suffused with his pleasure in the West Wight, are among his most lasting achievements.

> *And delight shall soar into ecstasy when a great shaft of late afternoon sunlight reaches the upper , bright against a sea of pewter, and my rheumy eyes seem to stare at the fields of Paradise.*

Priestley found such an Eden in his third marriage, to Jacquetta Hawkes, made official in 1953. He was now in his late 50s, and most of his important writing was behind him: his main task was composing 'opinion pieces' for the popular press. More 'literary' projects completed at Brook House included nine plays, the most important of which, *Dragon's Mouth* (1952) is co-written with Hawkes, and based on the psychology of Jung. Four characters represent thinking, feeling, sensation and intuition: one is marked down for death.

Jacquetta Hawkes later wrote *A Quest of Love* (1980). A strange mix of fiction and autobiography, this traces – as the blurb notes – *the climactic moments of the lives she has led in earlier incarnations,* in Knossos, Ephesus, Tuscany, and the England of Queens Matilda and Victoria.

It then describes Jacquetta's own sexual history, with a surprisingly frank account of her (at first) adulterous affair with Priestley: *nothing could defeat that polar magnetism.*

> *I revelled in the wildness of those days, telling myself that to be such a mistress was a finer thing to be than a wife. We made love indoors and out, by day and by night, in borrowed offices and flats, in the box of a provincial theatre and the garden of the Institute of Archaeology.*

The liasion was finally legitimised at Caxton Hall, and the couple were at last able to retreat,

to the marvellously beautiful setting of Jack's house on the Isle of Wight,
to begin a marriage that has lasted over a quarter of a century. We have
blessed that mysterious polarity that has never failed; we have enjoyed
one another longer and more deeply than any dream of love's avarice.

At Brook Hill House, Priestley wrote the rumbustious satire *Festival at Farbridge* (1951). Set in a claustrophobic local community, preparing for the contemporaneous Festival of Britain, Priestley targets pomposity and village rivalries, from his own backyard. The strangely sombre Huntley, Chief Education Officer for Farbridge, is supposedly based on his real counterpart, Arthur Hutchinson. One wonders just how closely the novel draws on the bureaucrats and local dignitaries of the West Wight!

> *A strange smile, the first of any kind Laura had seen him wear so far,*
> *illuminated the Major's face, like moonlight on a ruined city. And he*
> *spoke now as a man might from such a city, softly, coldly and with a*
> *kind of lunatic precision. "And in my opinion, Mrs Whatmore . . . you're a*
> *poisonous old windbag. And now" – the sudden bellow arrived with a*
> *grand sense of tone and tempo – "get out".*

J B Priestley: Festival at Farbridge (1951)

Despite his famed grumpiness, Priestley was known as 'Jolly Jack' to his close friends. The round of colleagues who gathered at Brook Hill House were perhaps not as dutifully serious as the Tennyson circle, but they certainly had more fun. Poet Louis MacNeice, the historian A J P Taylor, and Gerald Abraham, Professor of Music at Liverpool, joined local alumni Jack Jones, Curator at Carisbrooke Castle, Dr Richard Sandiford, and the Reverend Robert Bowyer, Rector of Mottistone with Brook. Taylor recalled their high spirits in a postcard to Richard J Hutchings.

> *When Jack Priestley was there, those were gay days. We celebrated*
> *New Year's Eve by a special party. Jack had a special bottle of drink*
> *concealed under his chair. We had a string quartet playing high grade*
> *stuff. We also had a conjuror. We had occasional music parties during*
> *the summer. The house was high on the hill facing south-west. Jack*
> *used to sit by the window growling "I hate wind". He went on enjoying*
> *the characteristics of the Island.*

On Sundays, Priestley would march his guests to The Albion and give them 'Dog's Nose', *an odd mixture of gin and draught ale, not intended for the sedentary.*

There were more elevated forms of refreshment. Professor Abrahams organised concerts of chamber music at Brook Hill House, inviting such brilliant ensembles as the Dartington Quartet and soloists Leon Goossens and Reginald Kell. Concerts were held in the large entrance hall, with some guests sitting up the stairs, and would stretch over several evenings. It was always a capacity house with the long approach drive choked with slow moving vehicles.

Jack Jones recalls how Priestley would introduce the players and programme, after which he would disappear into the large drawing room *where he would enjoy the music from the depths of an armchair, and the aroma of cigar smoke would be discernable.* On fine summer evenings, guests would spend the intervals strolling about on the garden terrace. Priestley looked back to this time with a sense of almost religious awe:

To watch the entrancing view emerge from the golden mists; then to pick mushrooms all afternoon; then in the evening to listen to the Brahms Clarinet Quintet; we were halfway to Heaven.

J B Priestley: Instead of the Trees (1977)

Here again is that almost archetypal feeling of visitors to the West Wight, that they are present in a waking reverie. It is a form of fulfilled indolence not often granted to humankind, and rarely lasts.

When the day was all sunlight and blue air, we would enjoy our drinks and lunch on sea-bass freshly caught. I remember Neville Cardus, among others, staying with us on a bright summer weekend, and after a few hours of it, saying slowly to me, "It's like a dream". And now it seems to me like a dream too, though not more than twenty years have passed.

Man cannot live by visions alone. Like Tennyson, Priestley eventually found the Island restricting, and remote from the passing issues of the day. He and A J P Taylor went out to local villages preaching the cause of the Campaign for Nuclear Disarmament, of which the novelist – who had undergone the horrors of the Great War – was a founding member.

Then in Taylor's words, *Jack got bored with the CND and spent more time in grumbling over the boredom of living on the Island. Then he quitted it.* In 1959, he and Jacquetta moved to Kissing Tree House, near Stratford Upon Avon. From Laureate to Bard! This was not without a keen sense of regret.

If we were so happy up there at Brook Hill House, why did we sell, pack up and leave the Island? It was all very well for us, living there, but our family and friends had to keep getting to and from the island. This was not very easy in winter with its sudden blinding fogs cutting us off from the mainland. In summer, with tourist traffic mounting up, you had to join long queues for the ferries and might be waiting for hours under the August sun. So we took pity on our family and friends and moved somewhere more accessible. But I am not sure we were right.

On a return visit in 1978, wrote a panegyric to the Island's *wonderful variety of form and colour, beautifully lit in summer months by the encompassing reflection of the sea, although he regarded the West Wight as ruined.* Like Tennyson the tourists has driven him away.

Brook Road joins the main **Freshwater Road** near Shalcombe Manor and Chessell Pottery. Turn left and after a few hundred yards, on the right is **Broad Lane.** This leads to Thorley and Prospect Cottage is on the left after a quarter of a mile or so. Poet and playwright Louis MacNeice (1907-1963), bought this – originally a shepherd's cottage – from the Priestleys in 1947. Born in Belfast, the son of the Rector of Holy Trinity, later Bishop of Down, Connor and Dromore, MacNeice attended Merton College, Oxford where he took a first in Greats. He spent many happy, literary weekends with friends at Prospect Cottage and it was probably the setting for his haunting poem *House on a Cliff.*

Prospect Cottage in **Broad Lane, Shalcombe** was sold to poet and playwright Louis MacNeice by the Priestleys in 1947.

Prospect Cottage today, extended, but still recognisable.

Indoors the tang of a tiny oil lamp. Outdoors
The winking signal on the waste of sea.
Indoors the sound of the wind. Outdoors the wind,
Indoors the locked heart and the lost key.

Outdoors the chill, the void, the siren . . .

Mottistone Manor dates from about 1560 and the Seeley family bought the estate in 1926. General Jack Seeley's extraordinary life is captured in a series of autobiographies which still make lively, stirring reading.

Back once more in Brook Road heading towards **Brighstone,** Mottistone Manor is about a mile past Hulverstone, opposite the elevated Church of St Peter. The house dates from about 1567 and was built by Sir Thomas Cheke, a *good scholar and a very honest man.* His cousin, Sir John Cheke (1514-1557) was a famous Greek scholar and tutor to Edward VI. He was later imprisoned by Queen Mary in 1553-4.

The Seeley family bought Mottistone in 1861. It was the architect Edward Lutyens who spotted the potential of an old barn on the Brook Estate, and said that half hidden by a cliff fall was the finest house on the Island, albeit *modest in manner.* The family dug out the original manor house in 1926, when it reappeared like an antique carefully preserved in tissue paper. The old barn is now the entrance.

General Jack Seeley was granted the hereditary title Lord Mottistone in 1933 for political achievements, and was Lord Lieutenant of Hampshire for thirty years. His extraordinary life is captured in a series of autobiographies which still make lively, stirring reading.

Adventure (1930) takes him through schooldays – he successfully organised an ambush on school bullies – travels to New Zealand and Eygpt, active service in the Boer War, military liaison work in Arabia, then command of a Canadian Cavalry Brigade in the Great War at Ypres, the Somme and Cambrai, until he was ordered home in 1918 after being gassed. Seeley had been elected as a Conservative Member of Parliament in 1904, but followed his friend Winston Churchill across the floor of the House to the Liberal benches because of his opposition to those who wished to end Free Trade. As Secretary of State for War, he did much to warn of the coming conflict in which he was to serve with such bravery. He died in 1947.

My Horse Warrior (1934), with drawings by Alfred Munnings, focuses on the stallion which saw him safely home, having survived enough near misses to rival any Hollywood epic. *One determined Bavarian, with a sword thrust right through his neck, raised his rifle just level with Warrior's near shoulder, and had a last shot before he died. Fear And Be Slain* (1931) is a series of adventures from Seeley's own life, which are *all alike in showing that "Safety Last" would be a better motto than "Safety First".* His role as coxswain on the Brook lifeboat is told in *Launch* (1932).

Paths Of Happiness (1938) finds similar consolations in music, horses, sailing and politics. Jack Seeley is a natural storyteller, good at pacy narrative, though his books remain unclassifiable. This is particularly ironic, as the Seeley family founded the first county library service in Britain, dispatching 'book boxes' to the remotest parts of the Island.

Corner Cottage in **Brighstone** was the home for many years of Island poet and historian, Richard Hutchings whose pioneering research into the Island's written literary past was published in *Isle of Wight Literary Haunts* and *An Island of Poetry*

No writer lives at the Long Stone, a Neolithic monolith erected at the foot of Mottistone Down above the Manor but Jacquetta Hawkes excavated the burial mound here, and her published account remains a turning point in Island archeological history. The Long Stone gave its name to a short-lived Island poetry magazine in the 1980s. It remains an enigma and still exerts a powerful influence over New Age believers today.

> *that old pre-Celtic lodestone, to set against the weather,*
> *a metaphor for shared adversity, a talisman never*
> *to die, setting our own skeletons against the wind.*
>
> Brian Hinton: Back of the Wight (1983)

From Mottistone Manor the road leads almost directly to **Brighstone** via Hunny Hill and **Corner Cottage** where Richard Hutchings (1922-1991) Island historian and poet, spent much of his life. In *Love Of An Island: A Personal Celebration* (undated) he recalls how, after an early visit at the age of eight, he had returned to settle in the Island in 1949. *I found work odd-jobbing with the Savoy Holiday Camp at Norton, cutting lawns and hedges and painting chalets.* One of his new colleagues suggested he take part in a smuggling mission, using an ex-naval torpedo boat. He was tempted but turned the invitation down. Years later, back from farming in New Zealand, this interest fuelled not crime but writing, articles collected in *Smugglers of the Isle of Wight* (1973/1990), and their legal counterpart, *Island Longshoremen* (1975). He began working as an agricultural correspondent, composing his pieces in a hollow of the hill on Headon Warren.

Hutchings went on to write widely, concentrating on poets of the English romantic tradition and Island history. His best books embrace both: *Isle of Wight Literary Haunts* (1979/1989) and *An Island of Poetry* (1979/1989) contain pioneering research into Wight's written heritage. I hope that in some small way I am continuing Richard's quest. He taught me the value of taking nothing on trust.

Emily & Alfred Tennyson: A Marriage of True Minds (1991) is Hutching's most achieved book. It doubles as a portrait of his own long and happy marriage to Elizabeth, who has herself turned both author and publisher – *Discovering the Sculptures of George Frederick Watts* (1994) is an excellent example of her work and other books are currently being readied for publication.

Richard Hutchings' *A Pot-Pourri of Poems* was published posthumously. I still find it difficult to be critically impartial about a man who devoted most of his creative life to exploring the literary heritage of the Island. As I wrote of *Pot-Pourri* at the time, here are the best of Richard's poems, in which the influence of Wordsworth and Tennyson inform a more troubled century.

His work is rooted in depression and retreat – *I am a fugitive* – from which, though, he extracts a rich love of life. A poem written during the Battle of Britain in 1940, recognises that such retreat is illusory and that the processes of history cannot be denied.

> *But here the haunting vengeance runs in the blood;*
> *And, though sweet, the unscarred scene*
> *Exhales a sense of peace and good.*
> *There is no division of the mind and retribution is hot.*
>
> Richard Hutchings: From the Country (1940)

In the best sense occasional verse, these poems never descend into cliché. The experiences of war are never quite expunged in later work – Hutchings fought with distinction through the allied advance in Europe – but the overwhelming impression is of a baffled hope, bitterly won.

The short lyric *The Price of Love* sums up the best of this poet's work, with not a word wasted, an honesty of response however painful.

Who shall ask the price of love?
Who shall assess the cost?
Who shall think to take account
What's given, what is lost?

These poems reflect a life given over to poetry. The title page of the book reproduces a photograph taken at Alfoxton Park – once home to Wordsworth – on the morning of his death, in the evening of which, as Elizabeth writes in her introduction, *Richard died . . . after a memorable and happy day on Exmoor.* Another photograph captures the fiery sunset over Tennyson Down, on the evening when Richard's ashes were scattered close to the monument to the Laureate, whose long stay on the Island he so carefully chronicled.

My contemporary review concluded that this discovery of poems – most buried away during Richard's life, and thus born with his death – enabled me to know better an intensely private person, who did nothing but service to literature. Would that the new generation of pampered post-structuralists, then currently building academic careers, attract so fine a memorial as this book!

The death of the author might have been long predicted by such intellectual gadflies, but here was the work of a writer no longer with us, but one who 'inscribed' honestly, well and with passion.

The pen surging in my hand
By no will of mine, I know
From the well-spring to the page
I make contribution in this garden earth.

On a lighter note, Richard's son Nigel helped manage the Marquée Club in London, and produced what was perhaps the first 'punk' single, *I'm a Mess,* in 1975. In one of the last photographs ever taken of him, Sid Vicious of the Sex Pistols, proudly wears the free badge which accompanied the disc when it went on sale.

On the corner of **Gaggerhill Lane** about a hundred or so yards back from Corner Cottage is Lower Hunnyhill Farm House. Locals attest to the fact that E M Forster stayed here while putting the final touches to his final novel *A Passage to India* (1924).

Through the village and on the right is St Mary's Church. The writer of the well known hymn, *Awake, my soul, and with the sun,* Thomas Ken (1637-1711), was Rector here. A fellow of Winchester and New College, Oxford, and Bishop of Bath and Wells, he was also a a writer of devotional prose and verse and is best known for the extremely popular *A Manual of Prayers for the use of Scolars of Winchester College* (1674).

In the garden of the parsonage is a yew hedge, planted during the reign
of Charles II by Bishop Ken, the prelate who refused admission to Nell
Gwynne to his house in Winchester and attended the monarch on his

North Court in **Shorwell** is a magnificent building constructed by Sir John Leigh in 1615. Algernon Swinburne was a frequent visitor in 1863 and 1864, meeting his cousin Mary Gordon there, and working in the library *the table strewn with big sheets of manuscript.*

> *death bed. It was also in this garden that he composed his celebrated morning and evening hymns.*
>
> Hubert Garle: A Driving Tour of the Isle of Wight (1905)

Novelist and travel writer Patricia Sibley still lives locally. Her novel *A Far Cry From Clammergoose* is set in Newtown and Godshill, and is the kind of gentle, undemanding read once de rigeur on Radio 4's Woman's Hour, where some years ago it was the daily book. A pet daschund features as a character in *Discovering the Isle of Wight* and *Discovering Isle of Wight Villages.*

Richard Hutchings was not the first writer to deal with the area's long acquaintance with the fruits of the sea. Fred Mews's *Back of the Wight* (1934) is still in print, a saga of every-day folk, subtitled *Yarns of Wrecks and Smuggling.* Brandy is landed, then John Cook of Mottistone – a carter – ploughs up a field for no apparent reason: *during the night the tubs were laid in the furrow, and there they remained for seven months, surely as queer a crop as ever was planted or seeded.*

Another rich harvest has been dug out hereabouts and Martin Simpson's *Fossil Hunting on Dinosaur Island* (1994) is a practical guide for those after old bones. Tennyson was there first, though. Emily's *Journal* for July 1865 reports a trip by Alfred and Professor Owen to meet the curate of Brighstone, who had an exciting discovery to show them.

They spread out their luncheon on Mr Fox's lawn and looked at the
great dragon which is quite new to the world. He never saw one so
sheathed in armour and thought of calling it Euacanthus Vectianus.

This is the first Iguanodon seen – alive or dead – for about 70 million years; the beast's skeleton is now displayed in the British Museum, while Tennyson's rests in Poet's Corner in Westminster Abbey, a mile or so away.

From Brighstone to **Shorwell** is a short distance, through Limerstone and into Walker's Lane where at the junction with Farrier's Way and Shorwell Shute stands St Peter's Church. No Island writer lived there of course, but its medieval wall paintings were once a form of story telling for the illiterate. The fine example over the north door tells the story of St.Christopher in a cartoon-like way. He renounces the devil, carries the infant Christ across a river full of jumping fish, and is eventually martyred by arrows.

Just across the road from the church is Oak Cottage, once the home of Jan De Hartog, Dutch writer of sea stories. He married J B Priestley's step-daughter, Angela Wyndham Lewis and they lived here.

Past the village Post Office is the entrance to North Court, a magnificent building constructed by Sir John Leigh in 1615. Elizabeth Sewell later used it as the basis of 'Emmerton Hall' in *Amy Herbert* – she had stayed there in 1835. Elizabeth Bull, whose father bought the house in 1783 built a mausoleum, with verse inscriptions to her sister, as well as the seemingly perilous bridge that leads up to the Temple of the Sun, high above **Shorwell Shute.** In 1863 and 1864, Algernon Swinburne (1837-1909) was a frequent visitor to North Court, the home of his cousin Mary Gordon – they wrote extraordinary, coded letters to one another on the pleasures of flagellation, an interest fostered by an education at Eton. She later recalled these years in *The Boyhood of Swinburne* (1917), and in her own poetry . . . *calm days*

When in the cloudless summer weather,
We wandered over those scenes together
Whose memory shall be a joy for ever
To heighten gladness, to soothe in pain.

Sketches in Recollection

The final phrase is particularly ambiguous. The poet worked in the library at North Court, *the table strewn with with big sheets of manuscript.* He first recited the following lines as he and Mary were riding their horses from Newport back to Shorwell, in February 1864. This is exactly that blur between the seasons, as depicted in his poem.

When the hounds of spring are on winter's traces,
The mother of months in meadow or plain
Fills the shadows or windy places
With lisp of leaves and the ripple of rain.

Algernon: Atalanta in Calydon (1865)

Tennyson met a youthful Swinburne at Farringford in 1858, and thought him *an intelligent and modest fellow,* particularly as he did not press any of his own poetry on the Laureate. Swinburne was later to parody Tennyson's oratund style, and his own work provides a dark shadow of just that kind of mellifluousness, stretched out to a decadent swooning. His *Tristesse of Lyonesse* (1882) remakes the Laureate's *Idylls of the King,* but puts back the rampant sex.

The full story of Swinburne's varied links with the Island – from youth to burial – is told in *Young Algernon Swinburne* (1978/1998) by Richard Hutchings and Dr Raymond Turley, who has written many learned articles about the Island's rich cultural past. They identify Mary Gordon as the great, lost love of Swinburne's life – she married Colonel Disney Leith – from clues scattered in his poem *The Triumph of Time,* probably written in late 1864.

> *Now, you are twain, you are cloven apart,*
> *Flesh of his flesh, but heart of my heart;*
> *And deep in one is the bitter root,*
> *And sweet for one is the lifelong flower.*

He later wrote of being *so happy and unhappy as a child and youth* on the Island. Shorwell provided the latter emotion, and it is imbued deep into the landscape. The pain here is neither sweet nor welcome.

> *The low downs lean to the sea; the stream,*
> *One loose thin pulseless tremulous vein,*
> *Rapid and vivid and dumb as a dream,*
> *Works downward, sick of the sun and the rain;*
> *No wind is rough with the rank rare flowers;*
> *The sweet sea, mother of love and hours,*
> *Shudders and shines as the grey winds gleam,*
> *Turning her smile to a fugitive pain.*

This could only be the stream that runs through the village on its way to the sea, *vivid* because it was stained with red minerals, as indeed, it still is today.

From Shorwell by way of **Farriers Way, Sandy Way** and **Kingston Road** heading towards **Chale,** Kingston Rectory is on the left. When Hubert Garle was in residence here in 1898, he recalls watching an ancient mummer's play and wrote about it in his book *A Driving Tour of the Isle of Wight* (1905). His account is priceless, both for its scholarship and its humour.

> *The company was generally composed of eight, or nine, raised from the surrounding farms, with a few fishermen. Their costumes were, to say the least, somewhat grotesque; one, representing a Turk, wore a paper suit of many colours; others were dressed in garments of stronger material, and wisely so, too, as they had to stand a good deal of knocking about; 'King George' carried a sword, a weapon evidently obtained from some wreck on the neighbouring shore; a soldier sported a red coat which, judging from its cut, had done more duty in the chase than on the battlefield; Father Christmas, with his wife, a doctor, a Great Head, with one or two beggars, completed the cast.*

Here was genuine folk-art. Here too was a community where *old men have told me it was unsafe for one man to plough alone, owing to the danger of being taken off by the press gang.*

Chapter Three
Billingham, Chale, Niton, St Lawrence & Ventnor

Turn into Kennels Lane where Kingston Road becomes Emmett Hill and after a mile Billingham Manor is on the right. This is the Killington Manor of Shane Leslie's – *A Ghost in the Isle of Wight* (1929). The presence of the ghost is accompanied by the scent of lilies. The same story was recounted, as literal fact, by J B Priestley who bought the 17th century Manor for £2,000 in 1933, and on its high, flat roof built himself a study *like the bridge of a ship,* overlooking Godshill. Here he pounded out innumerable articles, plays and novels. *English Journey* (1934) records his first impressions of the place, *English south country at its best in miniature – Lilliputian downs and all – with an Island quality added, a lightening of the horizon.* Its population consists of *an amiable and slow peasantry* who rise to a crisis and, *elderly gentlefolk* tucked away in charming manor

Billingham Manor. J B Priestley paid £2000 for the 17th century house in 1933.

houses. Now Priestley – neither old nor gentle – had joined their ranks. The approach of war seemed to deepen Priestley's concerns and this was reflected in his second volume of autobiography, *Rain Over Godshill* (1939) and in his strange drama *Johnson Over Jordan* (1941).

> *The rain had stopped and somewhere at the other side of the house there may be the beginnings of a watery sunset. Here it is all a vague and green pulpiness; you feel you could take the hills between your hands and wring green water out of them. Away beyond the tall elms, Godshill has clean vanished, perhaps for good, having had enough of our time. So come, away.*
>
> J B Priestley: Rain Over Godshill (1939)

Like Tennyson before him, fellow writers were drawn across the Solent to meet him. Alfred Noyes' autobiography *Two Worlds for Memory* (1953) gives an ironic account of this period, of H G Wells (1866-1946) pointedly falling asleep when Priestley began to discuss 'the writer's craft', or of Priestley's dejection that the advance sales of his latest book were only about 100,000 copies. He told Noyes that he would get the 'big guns' behind his work: Noyes was shortly afterwards granted a glimpse into what he meant.

> *Priestley had come over with Hugh Walpole (1884-1941). He told me that one of their publishers was flying down to the Island that day. Hamish Hamilton's plane (he flew it himself) appeared in the sky, circling above our tennis court. Never before or since has a publisher looped the loop over my head, but then, as Mrs Priestley had remarked, "it's all relative, isn't it"*
>
> Alfred Noyes: Two Worlds For Memory (1953)

Billingham was requisitioned by the army in 1940 and was home to seventeen different regiments in just the first six months of the war. When finally allowed to return in 1946, many of the family's personal belongings were missing, a particularly contemptuous way to treat a man whose broadcasts – *Postscripts* (1940) – had been so vital a part of the war effort.

Priestley's radio talks centred on the normality of life disrupted: the Cowes paddle steamer *Gracie Fields* sent to Dunkirk in an extension to hell, or Island farm labourers – and the normally deskbound writer – seconded to the Local Defence Volunteers. On St Catherine's Down,

> *somewhere behind that vague silveriness, there was a sound as if gigantic doors were being slammed to. There was the rapid stabbing noise of anti-aircraft batteries, and far away the rapping of machine guns. Then the sirens went, in our two nearest towns, as if all that part of the darkened countryside were screaming, like a vast trapped animal, were screaming at us.*

For a man whose image was that of a plain thinker, Priestley was obsessed with the numinous, with just this kind of dark vision. The theories of Gurdjieff, together with his pupil and expositor P D Ouspensky, and the philosopher J W Dunne, lie behind Priestley's four 'time' plays, three of which – *Time and the Conways* (1937), *I Have Been Here Before* (1937) and *The Linden Tree* (1948) – were written at Billingham.

The search for insight also underpins his dream of the birds, which concludes *Rain Upon Godshill* . . . It begins with Priestley standing, godlike, on the top of a high tower, watching a *vast aerial river* of all the birds in the world. Time speeds up like a fairground carousel, until the horrified observer sees generations of birds flutter into life, mate, weaken and die; a nightmare of existential terror equal in its numbed despair to anything written by Jean Paul Sartre. This is a far cry from the essayist of *Delight.*

> *Wings grew only to crumble; bodies were sleek and then, in a flash, bled and shrivelled; and death struck everywhere at every second. It would be better if not one of them, if not one of us all, had been born, if the struggle lasted forever.*

The use of the word *us* gives the game away. Priestley is talking about human – not merely animal existence. This is the great question of all religions. Why are we here? And he answers it, at least to his own satisfaction.

The pace quickens still more, so that Priestley sees nothing but a blur, *an enormous plain sown with feathers.* He centres on a rhythm at the heart of things, easily recognised as akin to both ancient ritual and modern science, and also – curiously – the most sexually charged writing that Priestley (a noted philanderer) ever committed to paper.

> *Flickering through the bodies themselves, there now passed a sort of white flame, trembling, dancing, then hurrying on; and as soon as I saw it I knew that this white flame was life itself, the very quintessence of being; and then it came to me, in a rocket-burst of ecstasy, that nothing mattered, that nothing could ever matter, because nothing else was real, but this quivering and hurrying lambency of being. Birds, men, or creatures not yet shaped or coloured, all were of no account except so far as this flame of life travelled through them.*

He draws here on dangerous visions yet through them, Priestley came to self-awareness. *I had never felt such deep happiness, and if I have not kept that happiness with me, as an inner atmosphere and a sanctuary for the heart, that is because I am a weak and foolish man who allows the mad world to come trampling in, destroying every green shoot of wisdom. Nevertheless, I have not been quite the same man since.* It is surely no coincidence, that this waking dream – as psychedelic as anything seen during the Island pop music festivals – takes place near Godshill, where Christianity and Celtic mysteries entwine.

It is an energy field which I myself have located in that same place.

> *. . . At the hidden terminus of both ancient leys and Christian sacrifice, I look*
> *at last on God's countryside, the man stitched book*
> *of fields and the eternal sea, undermining, undermining,*
> *I catch my breath at this timeless sense of hidden timing.*
>
> Brian Hinton: Back of the Wight (1984)

Priestley spent the bitterly cold winter of 1946/7 barricaded in Billingham, eating and sleeping in one small room and working on the play *The Linden Tree* for ten days until it was finished. *I lived with the Linden family*, he later wrote. Priestley's political career had run aground when he was defeated as propective Member of Parliament for Cambridge:

he was about to meet Jacquetta Hawkes during a holiday in Mexico. It was time to move on, five miles to the west, to Brook Hill House.

Late in 1959 Priestley left the Isle of Wight altogether and went to live in Alveston, just outside Stratford-upon-Avon. in Warwickshire.

Back now to **Beckford Cross, Emmett Hill** and thence to **Chale.** Rudyard Kipling made two private visits to the Island. In July 1891, he stayed in Chale with his literary agent and close friend Wolcott Baleister, and with Wolcott's elder sister Carrie, who he was subsequently to marry. In January 1920, Kipling and his wife made a sentimental return journey to the Island to visit Freshwater.

Gotten Manor was home between the two World Wars to Elspeth Champs-Communal, editor of Vogue, and a keen devotee of the works of Georgei Ivanovitch Gurdjieff (1874-1949). Visitors included Peter Brook, the visionary theatre director, and J Crawford Fitch, author of *Mediterranean Moods,* and many other travel books.

From Chale it is easy to find **Blackgang Chine.** A 19th century traveller captured the natural violence of the land here. *It seems as if the cliff has been broken, torn apart, leaving narrow valleys or glens, with steep rock walls on each side. Steep as the rocks are, trees have found room to grow, and all the way up to the top are covered with flowering plants and ferns.*

Aubrey de Selincourt found on a visit sixty years later that Blackgang – its very name suggestive of ruffians – *was now protected by a hotel, a museum (with a dead whale in it) and a sixpenny toll.* The steps stop abruptly, and there is a hundred foot drop to the beach below. *No smuggler, for all his dirks and pistols, the rings in his ears and tassels on his cap, could carry a load of barrels up the gorge now, even if he paid sixpence to the dead whale.*

Blue slipper clay ensures that this landscape is forever provisional. *One day the whale himself will be tumbled down, to roll his skeleton flukes in the surge.*

In 1864, Charles Letts of pocket diary fame had a temple erected to mark the tercentenary of William Shakespeare's birth.

The novelist George Eliot (1819-1880) stayed in **Niton** for a week during June 1863. She thought the village *the prettiest place in all the island.* It reminded her of Jersey, *in its combination of luxuriant greenth with the delights of a sandy beach* she wrote to George Lewes (1817-1878) her would-be husband, and author of the still valuable *Life of Goethe* which she had helped research in 1855. She went on

> *We have a flower garden just round us, and then a sheltered grassy walk, on which the sun shines through the best part of the day; and then a wide meadow, and beyond that trees and the sea. Our landlady has cows, and we get the quintessence of cream – excellent bread and butter also, and a young lady, with a large crinoline, to wait upon us – all for 25s per week.*

Virginia Woolf (1882-1941) visited the village in 1912 with her sister, the painter Vanessa Bell (1879-1961). It was during this holiday that Virginia decided to accept Leonard Woolf's proposal of marriage. She married him later that same year and five years later in 1917, they founded the Hogarth Press.

On the corner of **Laceys Lane** is a thatched house called Nutkins. Aubrey de Selincourt, travel writer and children's author lived here. His sister married A A Milne

Nutkins, on the corner of **Lacey's Lane, Niton** was the home of travel and children's writer Aubrey de Selincourt.

(1882-1956), whose son Christopher (Robin) married his cousin, Aubrey's daughter. Milne was the author of *When We Were Very Young* (1924), *Winnie-the-Pooh* (1926), *Now We Are Six* (1927) and *The House at Pooh Corner* (1928).

In *Storms of Ocean* (1923), de Selincourt wrote about the road through the undercliff as if it were drawn from a sinister fairy tale.

> *Trees darken it. Close behind them, on the landward side, is the cliff, perhaps a hundred and fifty feet high, mottled grey, a sheer wall; to seaward are more trees, thick and dark, with gaps between through which you have glimpses of the land tumbling away in smooth mounded heaps to the sea. Stone walls edge the wood; the stones are green with damp. The ground under the trees is black with ivy; the trees themselves are heavy with it – some strangled. I am always uneasy on the undercliff road, even in fresh blowy weather the air seems dank and thunderous. The trees are too many and too big; but in spite of their strength, the ivy has got them and will win in the end.*

Barrack Shute becomes **Ventnor Road** and then **Undercliff Drive.** Swinburne would have known this area well. Mary Gordon's grandfather owned a house called The Orchard here above Puckaster Cove. A rough sketch of the place by Lady Gordon was turned by J M W Turner into his *View From the Terrace of a Villa at Niton,* exhibited in 1926. Swinburne came back when he was thirty seven, in 1874, and wrote *A Forsaken Garden* in 1878. He imagines its grounds neglected and barren, as a metaphor for his own inner self.

The Orchard, Undercliff Drive — Once owned by Mary Gordon's grandfather. Swinburne stayed here in 1891 and wrote *The Sisters*

Another view of **The Orchard** on the Undercliff.

Craigie Lodge in **Undercliff Drive** was the home of Pearl Mary-Theresa Craigie between 1900 and 1906. She wrote under the name of John Oliver Hobbes. Originally called St Lawrence Lodge, it was renamed in her memory by her father.

In a coign of the cliff between lowland and highland,
At the sea-down's edge between windward and lee,
Walled round with rocks as an inland island,
The ghost of a garden fronts the sea.

Even the weeds that choked the rose garden *now lie dead.* At this time, Swinburne, never the healthiest of people, had become a heavy drinker. In 1879, he moved to Putney in South London with his friend and 'minder', Theodore Watts-Dunton, who gradually restored him to health. In 1891 he returned to the Island with Watts-Dunton and stayed with Mary Gordon, now a widow. Here he wrote his drama *The Sisters* (1892), dedicating it to Mary and including a prefatory poem about The Orchard, paradise restored.

Between the sea-cliffs and sea there sleeps
A garden walled about with woodland

Craigie Lodge is a handsome house at the junction of **Undercliff Drive** with **Old Park Road.** From 1900 to 1906, it was the home of Pearl Mary-Teresa Craigie (1867-1906), who wrote articles and novels under the pseudonym of John Oliver Hobbes. Her first novel, *Some Emotions and a Moral* (1891), was written on the Island, when separated from her husband and living with her father at Steephill Castle. In 1900 she moved to St Lawrence Lodge, as it was then known, where she wrote *Robert Orange* (1902), whose hero is based on Benjamin Disraeli (1804-1881), politician and prime minister and himself an accomplished novelist. She also wrote two plays, *The Ambassador* and *The*

Alfred Noyes, poet, playwright, novelist and anthologist lived at **Lisle Coombe** in **St Lawrence** whose grounds now form part of a rare breeds and waterfowl park. When young, Noyes had known the ageing Swinburne in London.

Wisdom of the Wise, the latter for Ellen Terry. After Pearl's death, her father renamed the cottage Craigie Lodge, in her memory.

A short distance away travelling towards **Ventnor,** is an austere, somewhat forbidding building that was once the Carfax Hotel. John Osborne (1929-1994) referred to it in *A Better Class of Person* (1981), the first volume of his autobiography, when he and his mother came down to the Island to watch over his father, dying of TB. They took the steam train to St Lawrence Halt, and passed a *gloomy, grey Victorian hotel called the Carfax.* Their temporary home was

> *a little 1930-ish house with a large derelict garden and orchard that went down almost to the sea itself. From my bedroom I could see out into the Atlantic for miles. The downland on the upper cliff was full of places to explore and trees to climb.*
>
> John Osborne: A Better Class of Person.(1981)

Within days, a black mist had descended, pierced only by *the flash of gunfire from the convoy attacks in the Channel.* Osborne played truant from the nearby school as often as possible, and was much bullied by the local children. His only consolation was his platonic love for Isabel, whose mother ran the Carfax.

Winter in wartime was a kind of stasis, a living death which matched the sad deterioration of his father. *The island was shrouded in silence apart from the whooping destroyers passing the island in convoy, out of sight in the thick mist. Something was going on out there and, whatever it was, I was missing it.* This sounds just like the aggrieved frustration of Osborne's character Jimmy Porter in Look Back in Anger (1957), but fifteen years before his time.

His father died soon after. His mother takes the young John in to see his corpse, and *as I looked down on him, she said "Of course this room's got to be fumigated". Frumigated was how she pronounced it.*

Alfred Noyes (1880-1959), poet, playwright, novelist and anthologist, lived at Lisle Coombe, whose grounds now form part of a rare breeds and waterfowl park. The poet's son, Hugh Noyes, who still lives there and runs the park, edited *The Isle of Wight Bedside Anthology* (1951), for which his father wrote an introduction: *few places are so suffused with the beauty and mystery of the sea.*

When young, Alfred Noyes was a friend of Wilfred Ward, son of the owner of Weston Manor – and had known the ageing Swinburne in London. He had not, as yet, crossed the Solent, until

> *in the summer of 1929, we made a short visit to the Isle of Wight, during which we explored a garden that had been described as the loveliest in the Island. Very shortly, Lisle Coombe became our own.*
>
> Alfred Noyes: Two Worlds For Memory (1953)

Noyes only discovered later that the house had once belonged to his second wife Mary Weld-Blundell's family, the De Lisles.

Here he wrote *Orchard's Bay* (1939), later republished as *The Incompleat Gardener,* a rich literary concoction which uses the topography of his garden as (literally) the grounds for a series of meditations on poetry. Noyes' classical learning – he held violently anti-Modernist views on literature – is matched by his knowledge of horticulture, studded with his own poems, and with the subtext of his religious self-assurance, *the Eternal Mind as it is expressed for us here in these lowly but exquisite forms of leaf and flower.* Noyes' own rapid descent into blindness following nine years lecturing in America in the 1940s, makes this all the more poignant.

Orchard's Bay concludes with intimations of *another and a more shining sea,* that of eternity. The prefatory verses are set in the poet's study – Noyes has brought Eden inside its book-lined walls – from which the lawns slope down to the sea.

> *All these wondrous flowers from an island garden, Cassia, myrtle, violets, roses, lilies, Take them. Let them shine on the shining altar, Where now, I lay them.*

Noyes resurrects the 'lost garden' of Swinburne – *who walked this garden ground/watched on this coast the long remembering wave* – and the brief flowering of a still earlier poet in this earthly paradise.

> *Near Orchard's Bay, the first white hawthorne bough*
> *Still calls him home to woodlands by the sea.*
> *Still from earth's breast, on bird-enchanted nights,*
> *He breathes, but with a deeper wonder now,*
> *"I feel the violets growing over me".*
>
> John Keats on the Undercliff

Noyes died in 1959. The author of *The Highwayman* and strange prose fables like *The Return of the Scarecrow* (1929) and *The Devil Takes a Holiday* (1955), lies buried in

Totland. In more recent times, the house has been used by Ken Russell for his film adaptation of D H Lawrence's *Lady Chatterley's Lover.*

Up on the **Pelham Estate,** almost opposite Lisle Coombe, Jean Ingelow (1820-1897) a poet with Lincolnshire roots like Tennyson, wrote *The Letter L,* rich in local topography;

> *. . . The Pelham woods*
> *Were full of doves that cooed at ease*
> *The orchis filled her purple hoods*
> *For dainty bees*

Alfred Noyes notes that *it was on the sand of our own foreshore that the fateful letter of the story was drawn.* The poem is so accurate that the place which inspired it can still be found to within a few feet or so. *You may sit there and be splashed by the same waterdrops from the little stream; and see the same flowers, the same birds, the gulls, the jackdaws, the martens; and the same sails at sea.*

When I last took a lone walk in **Orchard Cove,** I watched with an odd sense of companionship a lone cormorant diving for fish. Imagine my joy to read that night in Noyes' *Orchard's Bay* the following passage.

> *When the children were playing in the sand-pit, Orchard's Cove would wear a deserted look. On these occasions there was always one black cormorant swimming and diving, fifty yards out, and no other living creature in sight. He looked as if he, or his clan, had been doing it for a very long time – long before Swinburne used to swim there (as he did when writing Atalanta at The Orchard). Another cormorant, but indistinguishable from my cormorant as one rook from another, would have been riding the same waves.*

> *Long years ago, from the coasts of my own far childhood,*
> *I watched him ride the wave,*
> *And his way is no more changed than the wave's long whisper,*
> *Though a world has gone to the grave.*
> *He swims the unwrinkled swell of the opaline water*
> *Like a small black pirate swan;*
> *Then, quietly lifting a long sleek neck, dips over,*
> *Slips under, and is gone.*

No wonder then, that Dr A E Laurence's booklet on the area where he himself lives is titled *In Praise of St Lawrence: A Song at Twilight* (1988).

Steephill Cove can be reached by way of the Botanic Gardens. It was here that the last man left alive on Earth, Mark Adams, comes ashore in Alfred Noyes' strange fantasy *No Other Man.* He has been marooned in an enemy submarine and scrambles up the beach to find a different world.

> *Outwardly everything looked as he had known it and loved it for years: the fisherman's cottage under the cliff; the boats drawn up above the high-water line; the herring gulls clustering over their reflection on the wet sand; the dark heap of rusty-red fishing nets. It was all as lazily peaceful as a picture by Morland.*

But on closer inspection, a gull alights on the dead body of a young woman still sunbathing although the sun has gone. A notice pinned to the Royal Yacht Squadron's notice board announces the threat by foreign powers to unleash their new secret weapon on the world. "My God", he said, "I do believe they've really done it. I believe I'm the last man".

Steephill Castle was demolished in 1964 and a modern house now occupies the site. It was a mock-Gothic structure lived in for a time by Pearl Craigie's father, the American millionaire John Morgan Richards. He made his fortune from tobacco – another poisonous cloud! His reminiscences were published in 1914 under the title *Almost Fairyland*. Another writer to whom the Castle had been home was Mrs Henry Reeves, a popular novelist who wrote under the name Helen Mathers at the end of the 19th century. *Ban Wildfire* is set in the Castle and its grounds. It languishes in a few select libraries, unread. The poet Alice Meynell (1847-1922) attended a dance at the Castle in 1865.

John Keats (1795-1821) thought Steephill *almost of as much consequence as Rydal Mount*. For Edward Thomas (1878-1917), though, whose wife Helen, was from an Island family,

> *Steephill is not what it was. In fact, a great part of that double-cliffed seaboard called the Undercliff is reduced as far as possible to nothing but a show, with villa residences for permanent admirers and a very good road for the transitory. At Steephill itself the blackbirds sing as they probably did in 1819 in the ash trees and sycamores; the pigeons coo; and the pleasant turf is bright under the trees; then there is the "Castle", the hospital, the roar of the train, and the clatter of hoof and wheel. Travellers' joy climbs the ash trees and falls again earthward, but there is little traveller's joy upon the road itself.*
> *The best thing to do is turn inland, where stone steps help you up the cliff through a tangle of nettle, bramble, ivy, and ash trees, to Whitwell or the pure Downs: there woods are wild but threatened, and much of their sweetness has lately gone off in smoke where roots have had to make way for drains.*

James Clarke's *The Influence of Climate in the Prevention and Cure of Chronic Diseases* published in 1829 was the primary reason behind Dr Arthur Hassall's construction of The Royal National Hospital for Diseases of the Chest in Ventnor. It lasted from 1869 until 1964 when it was demolished. Ventnor's Mediterranean climate was considered ideal for those suffering from TB and Hassall did all he could to repair the wasted bodies of those admitted. He also wrote pioneering research papers on water pollution and food hygiene. He eventually retired to San Remo, where he befriended another Island exile, Edward Lear.

One of its medical staff was Dr E F Laidlaw who has written *The Story of the Royal National Hospital, Ventnor* (1990) as well as a more general history of Island hospitals. He now lives in Wootton.

The climate has also ensured the success of the Ventnor Botanic Gardens, fashioned from the hospital's gardens and whose car park now covers the original footings of the building. In *The Kingdom By The Sea* (1983), Paul Theroux writes of Ventnor as *an English resort in an Italian setting, the town tucked into bluffs and straggling along terraces and drooping from ledges. The way it cascaded from cliffs was Italian, and the balconies were Italian, and the tall windows too.*

Henry James described the town as *a formed and finished watering-place . . . reduced to a due degree of cockneyfication . . .*

> *Here and there it clings and scrambles, is propped up and terraced, like one of the bright-faced little towns that look down upon the Mediterranean. To add to the effect, the houses are all denominated villas, though nothing is less like an Italian villa than an English. Those which ornament the successive ledges at Ventnor are for the most part small semi-detached boxes, predestined to the entertainment of lodgers. They stand in serried ranks with the finest names in the Peerage painted upon their gate posts.*
>
> Henry James: English Vignettes (1879), reprinted in English Hours (1905)

In Ventnor, *you lose sight to a certain extent of the superfluities of civilisation.* However that orotund stylist of American English is not the only witness to record his impressions in print. In *Before Your Very Eyes* (1975) the comedian Arthur Askey added his own, typically perky comment, after an early paid engagement on Ventnor pier, *like the Roman legions a few years before me, I loved the Isle of Wight.*

A more recent emigrant from the United States is Lawrence Holofcener, a multi-disciplined sculptor who writes not only for the theatre – *Mr Wonderful,* starring Sammy Davis, Jnr. played Broadway in 1956, for example – but film scripts and books as well. *Britishisms* is a witty exposé of the gulfs that exist between English as spoken on both side of the Atlantic. His sculpture, *Allies,* of Winston Churchill and Franklin Roosevelt in London has attracted critical acclaim and substantial press coverage. He is also an actor, with appearances in shows like South Pacific, Kiss me Kate, Fiddler on the Roof, and Hello, Dolly, to name but a few.

Sven Berlin wrote about the closed railway station at the top of the town, using it as a symbol for what had once been.

> *The rails had gone, presumably back to the furnaces, and everywhere there was an unearthly silence. The ghosts of Victorian ladies and of Lord Tennyson brushed the buddleia with their long skirts. The sign for GENERAL ROOM was upside down, giving a queer dreamlike quality to the whole place, an Alice-In-Wonderland feeling enhanced when I looked across the platforms to the caves in the rock face. Inside one of them was a man painting a huge wooden swan for the Carnival to take place that week in the Town below. Swan of Tuonela perhaps, swimming on the lake of death and of past things. Who can tell?*
>
> Sven Berlin: The Silent Terminus (1970)

Berlin was a fascinating character, a friend of Augustus John and Ralph Vaughn Williams, one time member of the St Ives painting school, and a noted writer on gypsy lore.

The site of the former Ventnor railway station is in Mitchell Avenue, as is Hillside Cottage, once the home of the poet John Sterling (1806-1844), now a hotel. He came to Ventnor in a desperate attempt to improve his persistent bad health. He wrote the eight surviving stanzas of the uncompleted *Coeur-de-Lion* here but his own heart gave out

Hillside Cottage in **Mitchell Avenue, Ventnor** was home to the poet John Sterling who died in 1844. He was only 38 years old, and there were unconfirmed rumours of suicide at the time.

early – there were unconfirmed rumours of suicide at the time – and since then he has rested in the poet's graveyard at the old church of St Boniface in Bonchurch. He was only thirty-eight, a man that Thomas Carlyle had once called *the most perfectly transparent soul I have ever known.*

An anonymous Ventnor resident of the time remembers Sterling as having *the tall figure of a man attired in black. His features were haggard and sunken and for his age he stooped a good deal.*

Recently widowed, he was bringing up six children on his own, a 'new man' long before his time. As he wrote in a letter to his friend Carlyle *I tread the common ground into the great darkness, without any thought of fear.* During his final illness, he was cared for by his brother-in-law the Revd F D Maurice, Tennyson's friend. His parting gift to Carlyle was a collection of private verses, never since made public, *written as if in star-fire and immortal tears.*

In the **High Street,** roughly where Lloyds Bank now stands, Rose Cottage, demolished in 1932, was home in the winter of 1881 to Olive Schreiner (1855-1920) and her brother, Fred. An outspoken feminist and author, she was reading through the manuscript of her book *The Story Of An African Farm.* Published in a small two volume edition in 1883 under the pseudonym Ralph Irons, the book was an immediate success. Second and third editions quickly followed and it soon became known that Olive Schreiner was the book's real author. By 1900 over 100,000 copies were in print. A celebrity in the literary and political circles of the 1880s in London, she was admired by Oscar Wilde, became a close friend and confidante of Eleanor Marx and embarked upon an intense affair with Havelock Ellis. In 1911, she published *Woman and Labour* (1911) which was to become a bible of the fledgling women's suffrage movement. She died in 1920.

It was on the **Esplanade** that Ivan Turgenieff (1818-1883) the Russian novelist supposedly thought up the plot of *Fathers and Sons* (1862). Its tragic hero Bazarov is a 'new Russian type'. Turgenev had come to the Island with a group of friends in 1860 and had travelled all the way to Ventnor for the sea bathing. He suggested – one hopes jokingly – that it would be a good opportunity for them to seize Wight for Mother Russia.

At his boarding house, he dallied with a young German – *a little flirtatious, a little pensive – and another girl, a sphinx flashing riddles in the shape of telegrams.* While in Ventnor, Turgenev stayed at Rock Cottage in Belgrave Road, and Belinda House on the Esplanade, both now demolished.

Turgenev missed meeting the Tennysons in Freshwater, but visited them in Aldworth in 1871, telling them of reforms to the Russian feudal system then in progress (but which would not last). Ivan had been much taken with an exhibit in a Ventnor museum, an ancient ship's figurehead with the motto *Giovane Speranza,* 'Young Hope'. For him, this represented Young Russia. He also drew up a programme for 'A Society for the Propagation of Literacy and Primary Education' but he never followed it through.

Turgenev's visit to Ventnor forms the background to Richard Freeborn's crime novel *The Russian Crucifix* (1987). A young Russian girl is found drowned in a rock pool, and Turgenev helps solve the mystery of her death. Bazarov, a young Russian doctor and nihilist, saves a boy from drowning, but is swept out to sea himself: Freeborn postulates that he is later commemorated as the hero of *Fathers and Sons.*

From the Esplanade to the end of the High Street is about a mile when it becomes Trinity Road. On a steep slope at a roundabout, it meets **St Boniface** and **Leeson Roads.**

Karl Marx spent the winter of 1881 here, at **St Boniface Gardens,** and returned again in late 1882, a visit cut short by the death of his daughter Jenny in London. From here he wrote for the last time to his patron, Friedrich Engels about his fading health although *I still believe that with the help of patience and pedantic self-control I shall soon be once again in shape.* He was to die just two months later.

On the left is a tall apartment block, St Boniface Gardens. The ageing Karl Marx (1818-1883) spent the winter of 1881 here with his daughter, Eleanor. Ironically, the house had been built from money raised through the toil of workers at the Brown and Polson food manufacturing factory in Scotland!

Marx returned to the same address in October 1882, hoping that the sea air would help repair his damaged lungs. Dr Williamson of Southcliff, who attended him, had, strangely enough, also been called to examine the young Winston Churchill two years before. Churchill, who was six at the time, had visited Ventnor in August 1880 on holiday with his brother Jack.

Williamson prescribed a brew comprising quinine, morphia and chloroform. The apostle of communism and author of *Das Kapital* (1867) fretted about medical bills, but enjoyed the Island weather, free for all who could afford the ferry fare, *it was as warm as summer; the sky of a clear blue, with just some transparent white clouds.* Marx wrote for the last time to his patron, Friedrich Engels (1820-1895) from Ventnor, not about the pending assault on Capital, but about his own fading health. *I still believe that with the help of patience and pedantic self-control I shall soon be once again in shape.* It was here that he heard about the death of his beloved daughter Jenny, and rushed back to London, where he was to die himself, two months later. A E Laurence and Dr Allan Insole tell the whole story in *Prometheus Bound* (undated).

Back briefly in the **High Street,** the Library was once a concert hall. It retains its musical bias currently housing one of the largest collections of sheet music in the country. It is based upon the archive of Victor Fleming, a working conductor, who was also one of the many music composers associated with the town. Sir Edward Elgar spent part of his honeymoon in Ventnor in May 1889. During the occasion which had begun in Shanklin, he noted in his diary; *had to wade. Kissed her wet foot.* Forty years or so later, he scribbled a footnote *she remembered this the week she died.* More recently, Trevor Duncan the creator of musical themes for *Quatermass and the Pit* and *Dr Finlay's Casebook* lived in Ventnor, as also did Edwin Lemaire, one of whose 'serious' compositions has become better known as *Moonlight and Roses.*

Wroxall is three miles from Ventnor by way of **Grove** and **Ocean View Roads** and Appuldurcombe House is clearly signposted.

Francis Neville, Lady Worsley of Appuldurcombe, was a poet – the *Oglander Memoirs* attributes to her the line *Be what thou wilt* – and she is the heroine of Richard Nettell's historical novel *Naked to Mine Enemy* (1968). The action takes place in 1627, during Buckingham's ill-fated expedition against the French off La Rochelle. Francis falls in love with Jerome Brett, a Captain who has come to her attention by firing cannonballs at the stone wall which surrounds Appuldurcombe. *The wall was suffering. Blocks fell from the upper courses. Stone crumbled; portions collapsed as vibration loosened mortar. His trumpeter sounded a cease fire.* Nettell, an Island man, records that *this aloof, sheltered paradise* was first an ancient priory, and now an Elizabethan mansion, *a multitude of gables, roofs of lichened stone.* All was to come crashing down.

The present house was built in the 18th century by Sir Robert Worsley, friend of Jonathan Swift, and the process completed by Sir Richard Worsley who brought in Capability Brown to landscape the park and Thomas Chippendale to make the furniture. He also assembled a sumptuous art collection, later much admired by the young John Ruskin and wrote *The History of the Isle of Wight* (1781).

Edward Gibbon met Sir Richard Worsley returning from the Grand Tour in 1772, and found that from *an honest wild English buck, he is grown a Philosopher. He speaks in short sentences, quotes Montaigne, seldom smiles, never laughs, drinks only Water, professes to control his passion.* Something that his wife Seymour, whom he married *for love, and £80,000,* spectacularly failed to do (he was once awarded damages of one shilling in an action brought against her twenty-seventh known lover).

The house was hit by a German landmine in the second World War, and its roofless shell only preserved by the Ministry of Works at John Seeley's instigation. As the novelist, Rose Macaulay commented in *Pleasure of Ruins* (1953), *it had disintegrated beautifully in all the morbid shades of a fading bruise.* There was a vogue in the 40s and 50s for such premature elegies; their apogee is *Brideshead Revisited.* No one then realised that these relics of a feudal past would be restored to their original glory by the likes of the National Trust, rich entrepreneurs, weird religious cults or a National Lottery.

Chapter Four
Bonchurch, Shanklin & Sandown

Dr Thomas Arnold (1795-1892), Headmaster of Rugby between 1828 and 1842, wrote that *Bonchurch was laid out in the very way a poet would have imagined and a painter designed.* But for Henry James (1843-1916), there is something not quite real about the place.

> *Buried in the most elaborate verdure, muffled in the smoothest lawns and the densest shrubbery, Bonchurch is simply delicious and indeed in a manner quite absurd. It is like a model village in imitative substances, kept in a big glass case; the turf might be of green velvet and the foliage of cut paper. The villagers are all happy gentlefolk, the cottages have plate-glass windows, and the rose trees on their walls looked as if tied up with ribbon 'to match'.*

The Peacock Vane Restaurant in **Bonchurch** was once known as **Uppermount** and was the original home of the Reverend James White and his wife Rosa. They lived there while their own house Wood-lynch, was being built in the early1840s.

In a letter to his sister Fanny in July 1819, John Keats showed a similar ambivalence, though the boom in house building was still twenty years in the future.

Fit abodes for the people I guess live in them, romantic old maids fond of novels, or soldier's widows with a pretty jointure – or anybody's widows or aunts or anythings given to Poetry and a Pianoforte. If I could play upon the guitar I might make my fortune with an old song – and get two blessings at once – a lady's heart and the Rheumatism.

Keats confesses himself almost frightened to look closely, or he might fall in love. *As the world goes, chances are against me.* He had less than two years of life left to him.

Bonchurch Village Road transports the traveller into this verdant world of worn stone and overhanging trees. Opposite the Post Office, Bonchurch Pond seduces the weary to rest on its sun- warmed walls. The Peacock Vane Restaurant was formerly known as Uppermount and was the original home of the Reverend James White and his wife Rosa while their own home Woodlynch was being built in the early 1840s. Joan Wolfenden, who moved here in 1954, not only ran the restaurant but was the author of several books, on cookery, gardening and stitchery, each handwritten and illustrated with delicate watercolours. *Recipes to Relish* is one of her finest.

St Boniface Church was built in the 12th century to replace an even earlier building. In his *Historical Notes* (1931, revised edition 1945), H De Vere Stacpoole (1863-1931) writes of the annual service of dedication continuing through the Battle of Britain, and in 1944 watching the armada gathered for D-Day *athwart the whole horizon.* Thus,

on the Feast of St Boniface we saw the going of the last Crusade from these shores, by way of Normandy from whence, nearly nine centuries ago, the monks of Lyra set out on their mission to rebuild the Church of St Boniface.

There is even a legend that the saint himself crossed the Solent from his monastery in Hampshire to preach to local fishermen, before his martyrdom in Holland in 755 AD. The churchyard has a guide all to itself in Joan Gordon's *Here Layeth* (1959). Ghosts gather at twilight. John Sterling lies in the graveyard here, in the company of the Revd William Adams author of *The Shadow of the Cross* and Sir Ralph Chamberlayne, for whose burial Charles I was released for the day from imprisonment at Carisbrooke.

When, after numerous delays, Woodlynch was completed, the Reverend James and Rosa White took up occupancy and gathered around them some of the finest writers of the day. William Thackeray wrote in a letter of how *Little James White made his appearance yesterday looking very fat and chirping, though he has met with severe disappointments in his building speculations.* John Forster (1812-1876) wrote of how *cheerfulness and pain* coursed over White's face, and this was reflected in his writing career, drawing tragedies from the darkest Scottish annals while also contributing humourous articles to *Punch* and *Blackwood's Magazine.*

At Woodlynch, White's *good fellowship* drew to him the likes of Carlyle, Thackeray – to whom he was distantly related – Richard Doyle who worked as an illustrator for *Punch,* and Charles Dickens (1812-1870), who learnt *droll new games* here. That was not all. Dickens wrote to White that he delivered Matins better *than ever I heard it read in my life.* Such religious duties were not onerous. White was once called *the pleasantest parson that ever filled (or I should say avoided) a pulpit.* Dickens said he was *comically various in his moods, and enlivened by gin-punch.* As for his wife Rosa, *he is excellent, but she is better.*

Tennyson stayed at Woodlynch in 1846, during his wilderness years: *he was in a ricketty state of body; brought on wholly by neglect.* It was from this house that the Laureate's old hat was later taken, cut into pieces and presented as souvenirs by some over-enthusiastic Victorian ladies. But White probably cheered the future Laureate up. Witnesses have praised *James' quaint sly humour, love of jest and merriment, capital knowledge of books, and sagacious quips at men.* No wonder, then, that Bonchurch became a mecca for the finest writers of the age.

As Bonchurch Village Road becomes **Bonchurch Hill,** a lane to the right leads to Winterbourne, a hotel now but once the home of the Reverend William Adams. He wrote religious allegories and raised money through his writings for the construction of a new church, and laid its foundation stone. He did not live long enough to conduct the service of consecration, however and now lies buried in the old church, his grave shadowed – appropriately – by a large iron cross.

Charles Dickens had first visited the Island in 1838 when he stayed at Grove's Needles Hotel. He considered a return visit in 1848 to experience a sea tempest from the (relative) safety of Blackgang, but bad weather, ironically, halted his plans. In July 1849, he finally took up James White's offer to lodge at Winterbourne, and with his friend and *Punch* journalist John Leech, stayed in a lodging house in Shanklin before coming over to Bonchurch. He found the house *cool, airy, private bathing, everything delicious. I think*

Winterbourne in **Bonchurch** is now a hotel but in 1849, it was a private house and Charles Dickens lodged there. He found the house cool, airy, private bathing, everything delicious. He wrote part of David Copperfield here.

it is the prettiest place I ever saw in my life, and returned to London to collect his wife, sister-in-law, and children. Leech stayed at Hillside Cottage in nearby Bonchurch Shute.

Dickens' eldest son remembers that September,

> *continual excursions and picnics during the day, constant impromptu dances, and games and forfeits, and such like diversions. Performance of conjuring tricks, with my father as the magician and John Leech as his assistant, in the evenings.*

Dickens' magic show contained such delights as the 'Leaping Wonder' – a card trick – and a disappearing doll, concluding with a pudding cooked in the hat of an unfortunate member of the audience. The waterfall in the grounds of Winterbourne was turned into a shower – Dickens believed in the then unusual practice of regular washing – taking a cold bath every morning. He had the gardener cut holes in the sides and bottom of a large tub, into which he immersed himself. Dickens later had another shower bath made of such strength that it was known as 'The Demon'. Truly a power shower before its time! According to one local, Dickens' *"blunt and forthright manner offended many locally";* others noted his *"very rapid decided way of talking"* and his being *"excessively full of fun and spirits".*

At first the soft airs of Bonchurch seemed to agree with the nerve-ridden novelist – *the place is certainly cold rather then hot, in the summertime* – but autumn chills brought *an almost continual feeling of sickness, accompanied with great prostration of strength, so that his legs tremble under him, and his arms quiver when he wants to take hold of any object.*

At Winterbourne, in a first floor room overlooking the sea a hundred and fifty feet below, he wrote part of *David Copperfield,* chiefly the passage concerning the hero's long pilgrimage to find Aunt Betsy. Dickens wrote to Forster about his self-imposed regime, making himself invisible *until two every day. I shall have the number done, please God, tomorrow.* With the relief of any author who has completed a task on time, he then relaxed, *we have been sufficiently rollicking since I finished the number; and have had great games at rounders every afternoon.* Dickens left the Island for good in early October 1849, having settled *a tribe of bills.*

Edmund Peel who lived at Under Rock in the 1860s once met Dickens out walking, and the great novelist commented *You must like these downs as I do.* Peel replied, *Yes, but I cannot climb them as you do.* Dickens, who elsewhere wrote that *it makes a great difference in the climate to get a blow there and come down again,* smiled and passed on. Peel commemorated the meeting in his epic poem *The Fair Island* (1851)

> *And he is looking down into the dale*
> *On flocks and herds, and dwellings among trees,*
> *And slopes of yellow corn, and summer seas,*
> *And open promontories sheer and white*
> *Bathed in the blue serene without a breeze,*
> *He, whose clear spirit was a star of light*
> *To Nell, the wandering child, in innocency bright.*

Dickens becomes almost part of the Island landscape, another sun.

The Island also attracted its share of Dickens imitators. Most extraordinary, and still worth reading despite its heavy handed irony is Grantham Jay's Pickwickian saga *Mr*

East Dene was built in 1862 and Captain (later Admiral) Swinburne, father of Algernon, first rented then bought the house in 1841. Unfortunately, *the building now looks rather battered, and has an altogether depressing air of neglect about it.*

Percy Slipscombe's Visit to the Isle of Wight, being a series of humorous sketches on a recent six days trip to the Island (1873). Of Princess Elizabeth, the second daughter of Charles I who died in captivity in the gloomy confines of Carisbrooke Castle, for example, *"Is this a fit room for a princess to die in?" ejaculates our tourist, who is a devoted royalist.*

East Dene is almost opposite the entrance to Winterbourne. Dickens once attended a public tea here with children of the local school and noticed *a golden haired lad* of twelve, who played with his own sons. It was the young Algernon Swinburne and East Dene was his home.

Swinburne, though born in London in 1837, spent much of his boyhood at East Dene. One of his earliest memories was of being thrown into the crashing surf of Monk's Bay.

> *Its salt must have been in my blood before I was born. I can remember no earlier enjoyment than being held naked in my father's arms and brandished between his hands, then shot like a stone from a sling through the air, shouting and laughing with delight, head foremost into the coming wave.*

Captain (later Admiral) Swinburne considered this treatment a naval prerequisite but for young Algernon it was an introduction to self-imposed pain. *The scourging of the surf made him red from the shoulders to the knees, and sent him on shore whipped by the sea into a single blush of the whole skin.*

Algernon's family nicknamed him 'Seagull'. His novel *Lesbia Brandon,* published posthumously in 1952, has a young hero similarly entranced by the sea. *He would set his face seaward and feed his eyes for hours on the fruitless floating fields of wan green water, fairer than all the spring meadows or summer gardens, 'til the soul of the sea entered him.*

East Dene had been built in 1826 and Captain Swinburne first rented and then bought the house in 1841. Edmund Gosse described it thus:

> *The rambling gardens and lawns of East Dene practically shelve from the great trees in the shadow of the Undercliff down to the shingle and the seaweed. The view from the house south-east is over limitless ocean. Close by, to the east, is the wonderful chaos of the Landslip with its tangled lianas and romantic chasms, and to the west, the shores of Monks Bay and Horse Shoe Bay, with their groynes and fishermen's boats, so that on each side there lay an enchanted Tom Tiddler's Ground for emancipated children.*

William Makepeace Thackeray passed East Dene in 1832 and called it *pretty, but rather a cockney affair.* William Sewell (1804-1894), though, found East Dene *oppressively beautiful. It was so perfect that there was no scope for activity of mind. The beauty lay upon you as a load, and I never came out of it without a sense of relief.*

Unfortunately, the house now looks rather battered – it serves as a base for school parties visiting the area – with football pitches marked out on the green lawns, and has an altogether depressing air of neglect about it.

Algernon Swinburne rests forever in the family plot in the new **St. Boniface Church, Bonchurch.**

Algernon Swinburne rests forever just yards away in the family plot in the new St Boniface Church. Its foundations were laid in 1847 by the Reverend Adams who died before its completion in 1848. Captain Swinburne contributed over £600 to the building fund. His son was buried in the family plot in 1909 following an extraordinary funeral service. Algernon had spent the last thirty years of his life at The Pines, his house in Putney, South London, with Theodore Watts-Dunton, his lawyer. The latter was determined to carry out his friend's last wishes and wrote to the Rector of Bonchurch accordingly – *it was the express wish of Algernon Swinburne not to have the Burial Service read over his grave . . . the cortege will proceed from Ventnor straight to the grave; the friends will gather round it in silence, throw flowers and then disperse.* This did not go down at all well with Algernon's cousin, Mary Gordon and other relatives, who demanded a religious ceremony.

The Daily Chronicle reported the resulting fracas on 15th April 1909.

Life at Ventnor does not offer many chances of excitement, and to see a famous poet buried was an opportunity too good to be lost. The most enterprising gained standing room near the grave, and were only kept aloof by the constabulary. Exhausted tourists sat on tombstones, those with more energy trampled the primroses and violets in search of a convenient point of view. There is nothing definitely irreverent in a scarlet striped parasol, but it seemed out of place when it was unfurled to cover a lady in the front row wearing a cream coloured costume.

Victorian sensibilities were to be further outraged. The funeral procession appeared flanked by the stiff-backed family on one side, and decadents and bohemians on the other. The Rector recited the words 'Man that is born of woman hath but a short time to live' (somewhat inappropriate, anyway, in view of Swinburne's long innings), to cries of 'shame' and 'scandalous'. At least he missed out the words about the 'sure and certain hope of the resurrection to eternal life'.

Rikky Rooksby's fine biography *A C Swinburne: A Poet's Life* (1997) contains an account of the funeral by Helen Rossetti, (Swinburne had briefly lodged with her brother, Dante Gabriel Rossetti at Cheyne Walk in Chelsea) very much in the decadent camp. She came down from London by train with the coffin, placed in a luggage van. The Rector chants *like a carrion crow,* then to her horror Swinburne's remains are cloaked with *a purple pall on which was designed a huge white cross, and I thought of his verses, 'Thou hast conquered, O pale Galilean, and the world has grown grey from thy breath'.*

In 1910, Thomas Hardy visited the grave, and wrote his tribute to Swinburne, *A Singer Asleep.*

So here, beneath the waking constellations,
Where the waves peal their everlasting strains,
And their dull reverberations
Shake him when storms make mountains of their plains –
Him once their peer in sad improvisations,
And left us wind to cleave their frothy manes –
I leave him, while the daylight gleam declines
Upon the capes and chines.

Novelist H de Vere Stacpoole made **Cliff Dene,** in **Bonchurch,** his home for many years in the early decades of the 20th century. Cookery book writer Joan Wolfenden renamed it **Yaffles** after the local name for the greater spotted woodpecker *who likes to swing on the bones I hang out above the windowsill.*

It was at Hillside Cottage, then Hill Cottage, in **Bonchurch Shute** that Charles Dickens hypnotised John Leech, and probably saved his life. Leech had gone swimming after a heavy storm and had been dashed head-first into the rocks. He was put to bed, and Dickens rushed to see Leech, finding the poor man with *twenty of his namesakes on his temples this morning.* These did not work, and neither did an ice-pack, mustard poultices or bleeding from the arm. After all that, Dickens' methods seem positively modern.

> *His restlessness had become more distressing, and it was quite impossible to get him to maintain any one position for five minutes. He was like a ship in distress in a sea of bedclothes. In the difficulty of getting at him, and of doing the thing with any real effect, at first in a dark room, it was more than half an hour before I could so far tranquillise him (by the magneticism, I mean) as to keep him composed and awake for five minutes together. Then the effect began, and he said he felt comfortable and happy.*

Leech drifted off into a healing sleep, and the next day sat down to *a boiled fowl for his dinner.* Dickens joked to Forster about a career move: *what do you think of my setting up in the magnetic line with a large brass plate? Terms, twenty-five guineas per nap.*

Yaffles, formerly Cliff Dene, is on the bend in Bonchurch Shute, just before The Pitts. For many years it was the home of the novelist Henry de Vere Stacpoole (1863-1931). After the death of his first wife in 1934, he married her sister, and all three now lie buried near Swinburne. *A genial Irishman,* he was a ship's doctor, who set his novels in semi-tropical dream worlds. He was a best-selling author in his day, his greatest success being *The Blue Lagoon* (1908), later turned into a successful Hollywood film. Stacpoole enjoyed the fruits of his literary success, touring Bonchurch in his vintage Bentley and gifting the Pond to the village in perpetuity, in memory of his first wife.

He took great delight in his home, as seen in the name he chose for a collection of his verse, *In A Bonchurch Garden.* Ethel Hargrove describes Cliff Dene in its heyday. Being Ethel, she cannot resist the patter of fairy footsteps.

> *The house is approached by a carriage way overhung with flowering shrubs. Fragrant golden gorse is nearly always in bloom. In the recesses of the chine-like garden, the fascination deepens. A lawn fit for elfin dancers is framed by terraces of semi- tropical trees and plants when perchance fairy minstrels have whispered into Mr Stacpoole's ears as he framed thrilling stories of romance. The most picturesque approach to Mr de Vere Stacpoole's grounds is by Chimney Steps. They wind in and out in three separate divisions almost hidden by luxuriant foliage.*

They are still there but not recommended for the fainthearted. As Yaffles – the local name for the greater spotted woodpecker, *who likes to swing on the bones I hang out above the windowsill* – this was the home of Joan Wolfenden after she retired from running the Peacock Vane Restaurant and later the Bonchurch Bookshop in Ventnor. *The Year From Yaffles* (1987) takes the garden through the seasons.

The **Bonchurch Manor Hotel** was formerly **Hawthorndene,** the residence of 19th Century cleric Canon Venables, and historian and writer on church architecture

Tiny buds begin to come in that delightful green haze which promises us that the sun is in its way back from the deep south and that the miracle of the resurrection of the earth is about to begin.

St Boniface Church contains a fine example of Joan Wolfenden's exquisite embroidery. *The Four Seasons,* near the font, depicts a Bonchurch year.

The Bonchurch Manor Hotel was formerly Hawthorndene and the home of the 19th. century cleric Canon Venables, an historian and writer on church architecture. He ran a school from this house, and wrote guides to the Undercliff and the Island. Like Tennyson in reverse, he eventually moved to Lincoln. In 1860, he wrote of the village

the few houses which had been erected were mostly low thatched cottages entirely in unison with the scenery and the whole formed a scene of the most fairy-tale loveliness.

Elizabeth Missing Sewell commented more prosaically, that these same houses were *lovely to look at, but very uncomfortable to live in.*

The Pitts is a turning on the left between Yaffles and the Bonchurch Manor Hotel. It leads to Ashcliff which was formerly known as Sea View and was home for more than fifty years to Elizabeth Missing Sewell (1816-1906). She ran a school here with her sister Ellen, the painter. Montague Owen describes her books, including the bestseller *Amy Herbert* as *wholesome literature for girls.* She wrote many pioneering educational works, collaborating with another prominent educationalist, Charlotte Mary Yonge (1823-1901) on *Historical Selections* (1868). Her brother William was Warden of Radley

Alice Meynell, a poet and essayist of mixed English and Jamaican parentage and who died in 1922, spent 1864/5 at **The Dell.** Many troubles forced the family to move on. *I went round the garden and into every nook and watered the grass with my tears . . .*

Educational pioneer, Elizabeth Missing Sewell lived at **Sea View** (now Ashcliff) in **Bonchurch** for over fifty years from where she ran a school with her sister, Ellen.

College, Oxford. Elizabeth had come here to *live with the nightingales in absolute retirement,* but found herslf drawn into religious ferment. She introduced hymn singing to Bonchurch:

> *we were all very shy and at once gave up any attempt to practice beforehand. But we did sing, quaveringly I'm afraid. But from that day, music of some kind has always formed part of the Bonchurch service.*

For her pains, she was accused of introducing *foreign mummeries* to the new church. Her novel *Gertrude* gently satirised the determinism and religious fervour of those new adherents to the 'Oxford Movement'.

Current residents of The Pitts include the photo-journalist Michael Foale, and John Goodwin, local historian and dramatist. Goodwin compiled the witty *Bonchurch From A-Z* in 1993 and published a revised edition in 1998. He recently contributed a short story to *Gary Lineker's Book of Favourite Football Stories* (1997), as well as scripting fifteen radio dramas for the BBC. *Bonchurch in Prose and Poetry* (1993) demonstrates that contemporary writing in the area is still very much alive and thriving.

At the far end of The Pitts is The Dell. The poet and essayist Alice Meynell (1847-1922) spent 1864/5 here. A creole of mixed English and Jamaican heritage, she was now seventeen and it was time for her to be introduced to society. *I sported a dear darling mite of a velvet bonnet; violet, the rest of my attire black, so pretty.* It was here that she began to take Communion, praising the local vicar for *no apeing of popery.* She also began to meet young men: one embraced her at night *in a shadowy garden.*

89

Thomas Babington Macauley spent the summer of 1850 at **Madeira Hall** in **Bonchurch** writing the latter part of his *History of England* which he completed in 1855.

She became convinced of her own wickedness, as she confided to her diary. *Climbed into a field where I picked cowslips and tried to think myself an innocent little girl with no love affairs. But alas! My long womanly gown caught in every bramble, and I was obliged to keep my parasol up in pity of my complexion, and altogether I felt myself a faint, feeble copy of that innocent little Alice.* In her poetry, too, Alice Meynell brought her own sharp viewpoint to bear. As with Swinburne, and on the very same beach, the sea becomes a phantom lover.

> *What, I have secrets from you? Yes,*
> *But, visiting Sea your love doth press*
> *And reach in further than you know,*
> *And fills all these; and when you go,*
> *There's loneliness in loneliness*

Alice Meynell: The Visiting Sea

Money troubles forced the family to move on. *I went round the garden and into every nook, and watered the grass with my tears. The sun of my life set behind the down which hid Bonchurch from my aching eyes.*

Alice became a Roman Catholic in 1868, and in 1877 she married Wilfred Meynell. Their son Francis, who died in 1975, was the founder of the *Nonesuch Press.* Better known today for her essays and anthologies, her poetry nevertheless won her considerable acclaim.

Returning to **Leeson Road** by way of the Pond and **Trinity Road,** the gates to the driveway of Madeira Hall are on the left. Thomas Babington Macaulay (1800-1859), author of *The Lays of Ancient Rome* (1842), spent the summer of 1850 here writing the latter part of his *History of England* (completed in 1855) at Madeira Hall. *Here I am, lodged most delightfully. I look out on one side to the crags and myrtles of the Undercliff, against which my house is built. On the other side I have a view of the sea, which at this moment is as blue as the sky, and as calm as the Serpentine.* History is a myriad of such moments.

Macaulay's account of the writer's life is magical and quite unrelated to the fretful, money-pinching days of contemporary practitioners. Here he writes to his old friend, Thomas Ellis.

> *I rise before seven; breakfast at nine; write a page, ramble five or six hours through copse wood with Plutarch in my hand; come home; write another page. While I am at dinner, the 'Times' comes in, and is a good accompaniment to a delicious dessert of peaches, which are abundant here. I then take a stroll by starlight, and go to bed at ten. I am perfectly solitary; almost as much so as Robinson Crusoe before he caught Friday; yet I have not had a moment of ennui.*

Leeson Road climbs steeply out of Ventnor towards **Shanklin** passing Luccombe Chine. John Keats wrote his sonnet *On The Sea* during a walk through the Chine on his first visit to the Island in 1817. He drafted it in fair copy back at his lodgings in Carisbrooke, and enclosed it in a letter to John Hamilton Reynolds (1796-1852), dating it precisely – April 18th.

> *It keeps eternal whisperings around*
> *Desolate shores, and with its mighty swell*
> *Gluts twice ten thousand caverns*

Interpreting the poem, he explains that *from want of regular rest I have been rather narvus – and the passage in Lear – 'Do you not hear the sea?' – has haunted me intensely.* After this flight of genius, Keats' letter goes straight on to request a botanical dictionary, and for Reynolds to arrange the sending over of cups, basket and books.

Keats took a different view of the sea in a poem dedicated to the same friend, with whom he had hoped to visit the Island, and who was himself to live and fail there: here is the ultimate free market.

> *The rocks were silent, the wide sea did weave*
> *An untumultuous fringe of silver foam*
> *Along the flat brown sand . . . I saw*
> *Too far into the sea, where every maw*
> *The greater on the less feeds evermore.*
>
> To J H Reynolds, Esq.

On his first visit to the Island in 1817, Keats wrote that Shanklin

> *is a most beautiful place, sloping woods and meadow grounds reach around the Chine, which is a cleft between the Cliffs to a depth of nearly 300 feet at least. This cleft is filled with trees and bushes in the narrow*

part, and as it widens becomes bare, if not for primroses on one side, which spread to the very verge of the Sea, and some fishermen's huts on the other, perched midway in the Balustrades of beautiful green Hedges along their steps down to the sands – But the sea, Jack, the sea – the little waterfall – then the white cliff – then St Catherine's Hill.

One can hear Keats' imagination take fire, from careless descriptiveness to that sudden whoop of delight and wonder. It is almost as if his imagination were burning him up inside. Philip Edward Thomas (1878-1917) another poet destined not to see out his natural span of years (he was killed in the Great War) later described the Chine as *that huge cliff cranny, winding and full of trees, which they are now endeavouring to make more attractive by offering whisky and other liquors for sale at its entrance.* So nothing new there, then.

For Ethel Hargrove, categorically *not* a great poet, that process was now complete.

To visit the Isle of Wight without seeing Shanklin Chine is equivalent to travelling to Rome and omitting to see St Peter's; or going to sleep as we pass the Pyramids; though one tourist remarked to the keeper, "I think nothing of your place here; it's only a lot of trees and bushes, with a puddle in the middle". The next said, "I have travelled all over Europe and I never saw anything to equal this!"

The museum at the bottom of the Chine presented a new exhibition in the summer of 1997, on Island poets past and present. Opened by Hugh Noyes it contained a wealth of material from the likes of Tennyson, Keats, Auden, Hutchings, Gascoyne, and many more. The success of the exhibition with visitors to the Island, amply demonstrated that literature can be a significant tourist asset. Meanwhile the natural sublimity of the place remains.

. . . We meander down Shanklin Chine,
whose dizzying depths entrance, its steps fruited with light.
Giant artichokes seem relics of this healing scoop of time;
one could imagine dinosaurs here, resurrected in the twilight.

And at the base, refreshment. We soak up beer and gossip,
watch the iridescence of waves which break forever on
this festive shore, then climb back where Keats once sipped
life like opium, through holiday chaos to a walled Elysium.

Brian Hinton: Just Desserts (1989)

Hollier's Hotel (formerly Williams's) is on the left at the sharp bend as **Church Road** enters **Shanklin Old Village.** Henry Wadsworth Longfellow (1807-1882) the author of *The Song of Hiawatha* (1858) stayed here in 1868 and found the village to be *the quaintest . . . you ever saw. The landlady is a portly dame; the head-waiter, a red-faced Alsation; and when the chambermaid appears, you expect she will sing instead of speak . . . this is one of the quietest and loveliest places in the kingdom.* Asked to write a commemorative inscription, the American author obliged and this is now engraved on a tablet above a public drinking water outlet by the main car-park in Chine Avenue.

Henry Wadsworth Longfellow stayed at **Hollier's Hotel** (formerly Williams's) in **Shanklin** in 1868. He found the village to be the quaintest . . . you ever saw. This is one of *the quietest and loveliest places in the Kingdom.*

Oh traveller, stay thy weary feet
Drink of this fountain pure and sweet;
It flows for rich and poor the same.
Then go thy way, remembering still
The wayside well beneath the hill,
The cup of water in His name.

Eglantine Cottage at 76 High Street, Shanklin is at the top of Church Road on the right immediately before the junction with **Steephill Road.** An early visitor was Thomas Morton (?1764-1838) who wrote his play *Speed the Plough* here, which introduced that prude Mrs Grundy and Grundyism as the extreme of moral rigidity. The house has been many things: a land agent's office, bank and hotel. It is now a shrine to its literary heritage, with a special Keats room.

John Keats stayed at Eglantine Cottage in the summer of 1819 (from June 28th to August 12th) where he wrote *St Agnes Eve, Lamia* and part of his epic, *Hyperion.* His friend Charles Brown (1771-1810) moulded the plot of the verse drama Otho the Great, while Keats polished up the dialogue, to enwrap in poetry. The pair worked like the comedy writing duo Dick Clement and Ian La Frenais, trading lines, although the result was a tragedy in more ways than one.

More seriously, Edward Thomas pictured the poet looking seaward and writing *Lamia,* in which the English Channel was transformed through his imagination into the Mediterranean:

John Keats stayed here at **Eglantine Cottage** in **Shanklin** in the summer of 1819 writing *The Eve of St. Agnes, Lamia* and part of his epic, *Hyperion.*

Now on the moth time of that evening dim
He would return that way, as well she knew,
To Corinth from the shore; for freshly blew
The eastern soft wind, and his galley now
Grated the quay stones with her brazen prow.

Keats wrote to Fanny Brawne – the love of his life – that *the place I am in now I visited once before and a very pretty place it is were it not for the bad weather.* His bedroom window looked out over other house-tops straight down on the sea, *so that when the ships sail past the cottage chimneys you may take them for weather-cocks.* Here were *hill and dale, forest and mead and plenty of lobsters.*

Keats took his friend James Rice (1843-1882) with him, another consumptive *labouring under a complaint that has for some years been a burden to him.* More cheering was the visit of Keats' old friend, Charles Brown (1771-1810), from America whom he challenged to a sketching competition. The subject was Shanklin church. *He lent me pencil and paper – we keep the sketches to contend for the prize at the Gallery. I will not say whose I think best – but really I do not think Brown's done to the top of the art.* These were young men having fun, although Keats, a haunted genius, was already short of time. He records, though, his relief that with four friends *playing at cards night and morning,* he had been left no time on his own, and thus *no undisturbed opportunity to write.*

And yet, when they left him alone, his thoughts returned to Fanny Brawne:

> *I am now at a very pleasant cottage window, looking on to a beautiful hilly country, with a glimpse of the sea; the morning is very fine. I do not know how elastic my spirit might be or what pleasure I might have in living here and writing and wandering as free as a stag about this beautiful coast if the remembrance of you did not weigh so upon me.*

Keats wrote another letter to Fanny, too passionate to send, and spent each day *sprawling some blank verse* or *tagging some rhymes.* He found the landlady's voice overbearing but managed to ignore it long enough to complete the second version of his *Bright Star* sonnet, with its haunting picture of the sea at night.

> *The moving waters at their priestlike task*
> *Of pure ablution round earth's human shores*

The sonnet ends with a wishful hope, *pillow'd upon my fair love's ripening breast,* which was so far from being the case. Fanny reproved him for sending such passionate letters and mentioned that she was going out late at night in London, dancing.

All this fed into Keats' own mood of nervous aggression, captured in the luxuriant evil of *Lamia,* and the mood of the final letter to Fanny Brawne he posted from the Island. He was encased in a *little coffin* of a room (not a quote often used by Isle of Wight Tourism), and had begun

> *to hate the very posts there – the voice of the old lady over the way was getting a great plague. The fisherman's face never altered any more than our black teapot – the knob, however, was knocked off to my little relief. I am getting a great dislike of the picturesque, and can only relish it over by seeing you enjoy it . . .*

In what seems ominously like a precursor of the consumption that was ultimately to kill him, he complained that hot, dank sea- infused air collected and stagnated at Shanklin, taking on *an idiosyncrasy altogether enervating and weakening as a city smoke.* To complete this catalogue of woe, he also found that the scenery *did not take my cockney maidenhead.*

Keats left for Winchester, where he would compose the great *Odes to Autumn and Melancholy* (1818) and the *Fall of Hyperion* (1820). The closest he ever came to reaquainting himself with the Island was a year later when becalmed off Yarmouth on what was to be his final journey, to Rome.

Hope Road leads to the seafront. In 1858 there were houses at the far end of the Esplanade. One of these, Norfolk House, is where Charles Darwin stayed and wrote *we think this is the nicest sea-side place which we have ever seen, and we like Shanklin better than other sea-side spots on the south coast of the Island.* At the time, he was working on *Origin of Species* (1859).

In 1863, while still an undergraduate at Balliol College, Oxford, the poet Gerard Manley Hopkins (1844-1889) spent two months of the long summer vacation in Shanklin with his parents. The study of classical texts gave way to his delight in Nature: there is nothing wearying here.

The sea is brilliantly coloured and always calm, bathing delightful, horses and boats to be obtained, walks wild and beautiful, sketches charming, walking tours and excursions, poetic downs, the lovely Chine, fine cliffs, everything (except odious Fashionables). My brothers catch us shrimps, prawns and lobsters, and keep aquariums.

He made miniature pencil sketches of the local landscape, showing a precision of eye that would be bodied forth in his mature verse. *The present fury is the ash, and perhaps barley and two shapes of growth in leaves and one in tree boughs and also a confirmation of fine weather cloud.*

In the summer of 1866, Hopkins rejoined his family in Shanklin and confessed to one of his brothers that he had converted to the Roman Catholic faith. *He forced it from me by questions.* He again sketched the local landscape, and did some desultory reading.

There could not be a greater contrast with another man of the cloth, the Reverend Francis Kilvert (1840-1879) who first visited Shanklin in 1874. He arrived at the railway station to be met by his hostess, Mrs Coles of Newstead who turned up in a wheelchair given to her by the Duchess of Norfolk. Kilvert confides in his *Diary* (1938/40), in his usual chatty style, that

At Shanklin one has to adopt the detestable custom of bathing in drawers. If ladies don't like to see men naked, why don't they keep away from the sight? Today I had a pair of drawers given me which I could not keep on. The rough waves stripped them off and tore them down around my ankles. While thus fettered I was seized and flung down by a heavy sea which retreating suddenly left me naked on the sharp shingle from which I rose streaming with blood. After this I took the wretched and dangerous rag off and of course there were some ladies looking on as I came out of the water.

In 1875, he returned, and showed a love of life and an unclerical delight in young women, the two motifs which echo throughout his Diary, and keep it readable. As to the first, from the steamboat he captures a perfect day, *the Island smiling in the glorious afternoon sunlight and the tall white-sailed yachts standing stately up and down the Solent and flying over the bright blue water.* As for the second

One beautiful girl stood entirely naked upon the sand, and there as she sat, half reclined sideways, leaning upon her elbow with the knee bent and her legs and feet partly drawn back and up, she was a model for a sculptor, there was a slender supple waist, the tender swell of the bosom and budding breasts, the graceful rounding of the delicately beautiful limbs, and above all the soft exquisite curves of the rosy dimpled bottom and broad white thighs. She seemed a Venus fresh risen from the waves.

A different kind of view is captured by Paul Claudel (1868-1955) in *A Frenchman in the Isle of Wight,* translated by Violet Hammersley. The French poet's first published work, he was twenty one at the time, was written following a visit by himself and his sister in the late Spring of 1889.

We have lodgings at Shanklin in a small house at the foot of the cliffs, so near the sea that at high tide the huge breakers threaten the fuschia hedges which enclose our garden. There is nothing outstanding about Shanklin. As in every country town in England, the first objects which strike the traveller are the vast number of churches, and the potency of the mustard.

Life at an English seaside resort is one of adorable simplicity. Breakfast at nine, bathe at noon, luncheon at two, walk at four, flirt from morning to night. sleep from night to morning.

The view of the beach from our dining room window is one of feverish activity. A deep blue sea, all-of-a-sparkle with craft of every variety, bobbing heads, shouts, yells, windmill of arms, legs and oars. Now and then you catch a speck on the horizon – a man-of-war from Portsmouth, or a liner from Southampton setting sail for southern seas.

Another writer to bring a Gallic sensibility to *tiny* Shanklin was Paul Bourget, whose 1880 journal was translated as *Days in the Isle of Wight* (1901). He goes to church, *not a whisper, not a smile,* he finds that no swimming or beer are allowed on a Sunday. He visits the Chine. He even attends a cricket match.

Many of the men are in flannels, even those who are not taking part in the game. A band in village costume now and again strikes up an air from some French operetta, and above this gathering sparkles the lovely afternoon sun, shining on the thick verdure of the foliage and the grass, then far away in the distance steeping the outline of the darker hill in a cloud of mist.

Edward Thomas (1878-1917) also drew out this contrast between downland and the overarching ridge top, towering above.

Luccombe and Shanklin Downs make a good bold ridge against the sky above the sea The gorse glows on their sides. Seaward the ridge falls down in a wood, and at the edges the turf is shining with wide-open daisies and calendines in April. Before Easter much of the most admired and accessible coast is free, especially if the wind is strong; the nettles and thousand green things are pushing up as if there would never again be a procession of hard heels to tread them down. In early April the rooks are cawing in the elm tops of Shanklin. The gift of beauty does not look so profitable, and there are so many offering to provide tea that it is to be questioned whether the inhabitants live through the winter by providing tea for one another.

D H Lawrence came to Shanklin with his mother on holiday in 1909 when he was twenty-four. They rented Rose Cottage (whereabouts uncertain) and Lawrence had rarely been happier. With young friends, he went on long treks around the Island, visiting Cowes in the first week of August to see King Edward VII and the Russian Tsar review the British fleet in the Solent. Although Lawrence was only a young schoolteacher on holiday, the Island's scenery provided him with abundant impressions he would draw upon when he came to write *The Trespasser* (1912).

Arreton is a small village on the way to Newport, the main road to which can be found at Lake, mid-way between Shanklin and Sandown. The diversion is worthwhile to see St George's Church which contains a memorial to Elizabeth Wallbridge, the *Dairyman's Daughter* in Pastor Legh Richmond's tract. She was brought up in a farmhouse in the Arreton valley on Hale Common, not far from the Fighting Cocks Inn, entered service at Knighton Gorges and eventually died of consumption. Richmond chronicles her progress to this final resting place, a triumph of her spirit. His surplice was kept after his death and cut into strips in the sure and certain hope that bandages fashioned from such a good man's garment would heal any wound!

There is also a rhyming epitaph by Hannah Urry on her husband James' tomb. Gored to death by a bull shortly after the battle of Waterloo, Hannah clearly struggles to make sense of it all.

Gallows Hill leads to Arreton Manor and the Hare and Hounds public house. Local writer, Ken Phillips who lives at Apse Heath, has written the definitive account of a gruesome murder that took place near here. His book *For Rooks and Ravens, the Execution of Michal Morey of Arreton in 1737* (1981) is a suitably macabre account.

Michal Morey took his fourteen year old grandson out for a walk in woods not far from his cottage in the hollows beneath St George's Down. There, he sheared young James Dove's neck through with a billhook severing his head from his body. Michal had come well prepared with stout gloves and leather containers. *Gouts of blood soaked his shirt as the arms and legs of James Dove were hacked and twisted from the young man's body and buckled into the open wallets.*

A hue and cry was raised and Michal was soon arrested and Richard Norris was paid the princely sum of two guineas (about £2.10) for finding James's remains, now *a sea of maggots.* Imprisoned, tried and hung at Winchester in Hampshire, Morey's cadaver was brought back to the Island, immersed in hot pitch to help preserve it and hung in chains on a gibbet, where it slowly rotted away, assisted no doubt, by the rooks and ravens.

Part of the iron chains were retrieved by a William Joliffe and made into a souvenir pipe rack for use in a Newport hostelry. The gibbet post is said to have taken on a second lease of life as a floor joist at the Hare and Hounds, although Phillips is sceptical about this aspect of the tale. He concludes

> *In modern sociological terms, the illiterate Moreys ... would have been noted as a family 'at risk' and the ageing Michal's behaviour may have betrayed symptoms of paranoia or schizophrenia long before the crisis occurred.*

That said no one book can put paid to the Michal Morey myth: it merely serves to fuel further speculation into a story whose power comes from the essential mystery at its core. The very absence of apparent motive, and the gruesomeness of the sudden violence touches a deep part of the human psyche, far removed from mere academic enquiry.

Take the road across the Downs towards **Brading** until **Knighton** is indicated to the right. Knighton Gorges, a house of which only two stone gateposts remain, was on land to the left, now belonging to Southern Water. Elizabeth Daish of Seaview has chronicled the remarkable story of this building which at one time played host to the likes of David Garrick, Sir Joshua Reynolds, and John Wilkes. In 1821 Maurice George Bisset, who then owned Knighton Gorges, refused to let his eldest daughter marry a clergyman, and rather than have her eventually inherit the house, ordered it demolished. He himself died a month later in the gardener's cottage. So well did the workmen carry out their task that nothing remains at all, save the gateposts, to show where the house once stood. The whole place is haunted, of course. The ever-credulous Ethel Hargrove continues the story:

> *Urged by curiosity, I visited the deserted neighbourhood late one New Year's Eve. Being not an expert in occult happenings, I can offer no explanation. Was it long-pent up sounds revived by certain influences working in the air, or something as yet beyond the ken of mankind? A few minutes before midnight a flood of melody arose from the site of the former mansion. It was varied in character – dance music played on a harpsichord, Georgian minuet airs slow and stately, then a duet between tenor and soprano voices. At twelve the party seemed to break up, a pistol or gun was fired, dogs bayed, and the sound of carriage wheels was heard. Lights moved, till the dark night again covered the landscape and a New Year came into being.*

Knighton Shute becomes **Knighton Lane,** and then runs through Newchurch to Apse Heath. Ken Phillips of *Rooks and Ravens* fame, who is also the author of two books about shipwrecks on the Island's coast lives here. His latest *Shipwreck! Broken on the Wight* (1996) contains an investigation into the mysterious sinking of the P S Portsdown in the Solent in September 1941, concluding that the little ferry was the casualty of a British mine, adrift and unmarked. An own goal that left some twenty or so Island people dead.

Lake is the home of the prolific Carol Barton, author of some twenty or so novels for Mills and Boon, probably the world's best known publisher of romantic fiction. Written strictly to a formula and a deadline, surely a less romantic process would be difficult to imagine. Carol is now branching out into books for children. *Mystery Valentine* (1997) may be 'formula fiction' but Barnes infuses great freshness into this story of a 'Young Hippo Spooky.' The tale features the ghost of Valentine Gray, a Newport chimney sweep who died at the age of ten and whose memorial is in Church Litten adjacent to the Lord Louis Library in the town.

Sandown is the natural choice of many holidaymakers visiting the Island, primarily because of its fine sandy beach and sweeping bay. Regent Court, opposite the Library and Museum at the junction of **Culver Road** with the **High Street,** is built on what was once the site of a boarding house where Lewis Carroll stayed for three idyllic summers from 1875. Here he wrote part of *The Hunting of the Snark* (1876). Gertrude Chataway, then a child, *a girl with a boyish garb,* and to whom Dodgson was to dedicate the poem, recalled how the poet

> *would come onto his balcony, which joined ours, sniffing the sea-air with his head thrown back, and would walk down the steps to the beach, drinking in the fresh breezes as if he could never have enough. We used to sit for hours on the wooden steps which led to the beach, whilst he told the most lovely tales that could possibly be imagined.*

The poem is a heavily mythologised, and farcical (yet sinister) account of a sea voyage, which hurtles towards a shipwreck, and which draws abstractly on his proximity to open water.

He had bought a large map representing the sea,
Without the least vestige of land:
And the crew were much pleased when they found it to be
A map they could all understand.

Ryde author Cathy Bowern – similarly a pseudonym – published the *Hunting of the Snark Concluded* in 1997. The Bellman and his crew face starvation, almost provoke a mutiny, and their voyage comes to a mysterious conclusion. Bowern claims to have discovered a secret formula concealed in the last line of Carroll's original which transforms the whole poem, and this is contained in *The Snark Decoded* (1997), on the front cover of which the Mad Hatter confronts a Rubik's cube.

Cathy Bowern has already relocated *Alice Through the Looking Glass* to the Island with riddles intact in *A Looking Glass Sequel* (1993), published in manuscript with illustrations by local artist Brian Puttock. The events reverse the order of the original book. An extremely bizarre card game starts on a 'Looking Glass Pier', made into a giant chessboard. The language is a exact imitation of Carroll, pitched exactly at the point where nonsense turns into nightmare.

> *"I should see the Regatta far better", said Alice, pausing for breath, "if I could actually reach the boathouse – at least, not, if I follow the pier straight along it doesn't go there after all . . . but I suppose it will last. But how curiously it doubles back on itself! Well this direction goes back to boathouse I suppose – no it doesn't! It goes back to the dratted deckchair! I'm not sure that wasn't here a minute ago.*

While stationed at Golden Hill Fort, A A Milne rented the *prettiest cottage in Sandown.* and wrote a play, which became his first book for children *Once Upon a Time* (c.1920).

The strange residence of John Wilkes (1727-1797), a political agitator amongst many other things, and who leased a summer house in Sandown in 1792, has long been swept away by the tides. Wilkes was a strange, larger-than-life figure, in a gaudy coat laced with gold, high boots and powdered hair. Despite this, he was a man of great wit, learning and a fighter for human rights, he was also a notorious libertine and a member of the Hell Fire Club. Elected MP for Aylesbury in 1757, he was subsequently expelled from Parliament for publishing an obscene libel, the *Essay on Women*. In 1774, he was not only re-elected as MP for Middlesex but became Lord Mayor of London. 'Wilkes Villa' as his home on the Island became known was described by Wilkes himself

> *My villakin at 'Sandham' 'tis sans doubt,*
> *The quaintest cottage ever builded*

Here Wilkes wrote his *Memoirs* and many letters, with precise observation. These were diligently gathered by J Almond in his edition of the *Correspondence of the Late John Wilkes* and published in 1805. A typical example:

> *I have seen twice at Sandown, a dozen porpoises sporting near the shore, and counted 150 ships, principally merchantmen in the Bay . . . the landing at Ryde is shamefully neglected. I passed a great herring pond yesterday in an open boat in one and three quarter hours. All the winds were asleep, and I was fanned by not a single zephyr.*

In the grounds of the villa, Wilkes had a Doric column erected to the memory of his friend, the satirist and poet Charles Churchill (1731-1764). Churchill had dedicated his poem *Prophecy of Famine* (1763) to Wilkes and subsequently left him in his will all his papers and entrusted him with the care of his reputation. Wilkes' only attempt to further the latter was the construction of this column, long since lost to the waves, with its inscription to "The divine poet, the genial friend, the citizen deserving of his country's highest regard".

Hill Street in Sandown is the home still of Edward Falaise Upward (1903-), who might outwardly appear as different from John Wilkes as is humanly possible, but whose imagination is wilder still. Born in Essex and educated at Repton College and Corpus Christi College, Cambridge, Upward became the lifelong friend of Christopher Isherwood. Together they invented the fantasy world of 'Mortmere'.

Upward allowed the poetry anthology *Island Images* to reprint an extract from his short story *The Island* (1934), on its 50th anniversary in 1984. Its power is palpable.

> *Look across the real water: look, this Island can't be a floodlit cloud, can't be a daydream through which you'll slip to find yourself back on the job and under the poisonous eyes of a bullying foreman. One hundred and fifty square miles of it, and the sand is unarguably sand, the earth is earth, the limestone limestone, fluviomarine and estuarial, and roundly the real downs descend to the town, and the houses and bright hotels are crowding towards the pier, and the pier a pavilion headed millipede is toddling through the springtime waves towards your paddle-steamer, this holiday steamer loaded with the first visitors of the year.*

Thus the holiday island seems to be an image of what those freed from capitalistic demands for the sweat from their brows could be released to – a free life. *What weary imposture, what ghost-life, what devil's island in the heart have you allowed yourself to be cheated with until now.* But just like the end of that similarly surrealistic television series *The Prisoner,* when the door to Patrick McGoohan's flat opens of its own accord, just like the prison he has 'escaped' from, from which there is positively no escape, all this is itself illusory. The extract used for *Island Images* ends here, but Upward's original text becomes increasingly foreboding, the yacht club terrace *like a redoubt behind its semi-circular sea wall hides enemy cannon,* the pier pavilion *will bite your head off,* the gaudy amusement hall is

> *fraudulent as vulgar icing on a celebration cake, rotten inside with maggots, sugary poison to drug you to contentment.*

Fernside was once the home of Maud Berkeley, whose diaries written at the end of the 19th century were republished with their original pencil sketches as *Maud* (1985), adapted by Flora Fraser – Lady Antonia's daughter – and with an introduction by Elizabeth Longford.

By turns facinating and tedious, they do evoke an upper middle class social life, with excursions to Collingbourne Lodge, Spring Villa, Appuldurcombe House and Luccombe. Tennis and dances are the highlights, and little incidents loom large. After all, these are an aide-mémoire and not something polished up for public consumption.

We all set out for Carisbrooke castle in a wagonette, little Ruby Barnes and Edmund Neal – a most troublesome boy – sitting in the front, pretending to drive the vehicle themselves. When we got to the castle, there were so many wasps about the table that it was thought dangerous to trust me with the crockery. I was directed to entertain the children, made daisy chains in the shelter of a fortified wall. Wonderful picnic, barring an accident when Arthur Drabble got up unexpectedly, and the bench deposited me abruptly on the ground.

The most interesting aspects are the incidentals, the *Shanklin Spinster's Picnic,* and the *Shanklin Batchelor's Dance.* Maud herself writes about *dull hours* enlivened by writing her diary. They make a foray to Freshwater, but never see Tennyson. A foreign friend *splendid in furs and boas* visiting Seaview Hotel keeps the staff in *a perpetual anxiety.* One feels sorry for them, even a century later.

Dr Allan Insole, geologist and archaeologist, lives in Sandown and has published widely in his scientific field, specialising in the landscape of Wight and the west coast of Ireland. With David Burdett of East Cowes Heritage, he published *Discovering An Island* in 1995. Subtitled *A Roadside Guide to the Heritage of the Isle of Wight* it remains an invaluable reference book for those touring the Island by car.

The poet Edward Thomas saw that particularly melancholy sight here, a British seaside resort, out of season . . .

Sandown is more dejected. It ought to be packed up and stowed away somewhere for the winter. All the summer the poor little houses are wonderfully furnished with happy children, but there are none there to see the early gorse flowering in the precipices of sand and to pick the colt's-foot blossom and the curious pagodas of the mares'-tails. Day after day the sea rearranges the pebbles on the brindled and yellow sand and no footprint disturbs them. Every stone is precious while it is wet.

From **Culver Road,** Culver Cliff is impossible to miss. When seventeen, Algernon Swinburne climbed to the summit – without ropes – in 1854. He had been accused by his father of not being brave enough to fight in the Crimean War, and this was a demonstration of his manliness. He tried once, failed, and then began his slow ascent . . .

I was most of the way up when I heard a sudden sound as of loud music, reminding me instantly of the 'anthem' from the Eton College organ. I knew it would be almost certain death to look down, and the next minute there was no need; I glanced aside, and saw the opening of a great hollow in the upper cliff, out of which came swarming a great flock of seagulls who evidently had never seen a wingless brother so near the family quarters before. I was a little higher, when I thought how queer it would be if my very scanty foothold gave way; and at that very minute, it did. I swung in the air by my hands from a ledge on the cliff which just gave room for my fingers to cling and hold on. There was a projection of rock to the left at which I flung out my feet sideways and just reached it; this enabled me to get breath and crawl at full speed up the remaining bit of cliff. At the top I had not strength enough left to turn

Culver Cliff, Sandown. The young Algernon Swinburne climbed to the top without ropes in 1854 to demonstrate his manliness to his father. *At the top I had not strength enough to turn or stir.*

or stir. I lay on my right side helpless. On returning to conscious life, I found a sheep's nose just over mine, and the poor good fellow creature's eyes gazing into my face with such a look of kind pity and sympathy as well as surprise and perplexity that I never ought to have eaten a mutton-chop again.

Edward Thomas, less extreme in his life and his poetry, uses his Island survey published in 1911, to capture just this same sense of these chalk cliffs as a repository of menace and danger.

Away in the north-east the high wall of the Culver Cliffs are very white above seas of a cold, soft green, flecked with white. They seem now a fit home for peregrine and raven. The waves are not big, but that fleck of white is almost always interpreted as anger. it is the same wherever this effect is imitated on land. For example snow lingering here and there in paths and hollows on the hills, or on the dark yews in a hanging beechwood, or even the chalky scratching of rabbits on the face of the Downs, owes, I think, to the reminder of a foam-flecked sea the full wildness and severity of its appearance.

C J Cornish had been there ten years or so before, and found

a square-topped buttress of chalk, incurved and overhanging, with wavy lines of flints running from top to bottom. For fifty feet above the water the cliff was covered with pale, sulphur-coloured lichen, and the surface was so smooth and hard as to afford no foothold even to the birds, except to the sand-martins which, abandoning the burrowing

103

habits of their race, had made themselves nests of chalk pellets. The beams of the setting sun streamed over the top of the precipice, and against the light the tiny martins were visible, like gnats against the evening sky.

Virtually impregnable then, but Swinburne was nothing if not a masochist.

Chapter Five – Brading, Bembridge & Ryde

Brading faced the sea for many centuries, and the visiting Lord Nelson would have stared over a tidal estuary, like Wootton Creek today. The town was reputed to have been founded by the legendary King Alfred, and it was from here that he fought the Danish navy in 896. The area was eventually drained with the construction of an embankment but not until 1879. Ten years later, Paul Claudel writes of *a landscape misty blue as in a fairy tale. We arrive at Brading, a village of small cottages with tiny latticed panes. The signboards of two inns, 'The Red Lion' and 'The White Shield' welcome the traveller – inns where Falstaff might have ordered Bardolph or Poins to bring him a quart of sack.*

'THP', writing in *Notes and Queries* in 1858, describes how *entering the village on Christmas Day we were accosted by a ragged crowd of 'mummers' in gay dresses of shreds of coloured paper and skilfully cut pages of copy books.* The reader cannot fail to notice how a pre-literate tradition lacking all the accoutrements of written-down language predates Caxton and Gutenburg!

'THP' notes an addition to the usual crew, *a black-faced actor in a ragged smock, and carrying a stout cudgel with a bell on one end.* This Ken Dodd of his time, combines the roles of prompter, stage director and master of ceremonies.

Brading church was built on a pagan site, where we are told, giants' bones were found. Legh Richmond, author of *The Dairyman's Daughter* and *Annals of the Poor* was curate here from 1797 to 1805. There is a monument to him in the church. His most famous religious tract is today largely unreadable, overblown and saccharine: *it is peculiarly gratifying to observe how frequently, among the poorer classes of mankind, the sunshine of mercy beams upon the heart, and bears witness to the image of Christ.* Of course, the Dairyman's daughter dies prettily – *a sweet smile enlightened her pale countenance.*

The *Negro Servant* is even more alien to modern eyes, *"Massa", says he, "me not know what to say to all dese goot friends; me tink dis look a little like heaven on earth".*

Literary tradition lives on in Brading Waxworks, if only through a series of historical tableaux which include George Bernard Shaw, mounted on a pennyfarthing bicycle, surveying the cliffs of Freshwater Bay, and Tennyson in his study at Farringford.

Coach Lane on the left leads to Nunwell House. Sir John Oglander lived here from 1585 to 1655. He was imprisoned by the Parliamentarians during the Civil War, and his words took centuries to enter the public domain. W H Long edited *The Oglander Memoirs* in 1888 and F Bamford *A Royalists Notebook* in 1936. One of Sir John's highly practical letters to Lady Oglander written from prison thus survives:

> *All that I desire of you is to beare it with a good courage and not by your gryfe to lett our enemys see you cast down. My black swyte begins to*

be torne wherefore pray go to ye trounke in ye cellar where the tobaccoe is. Send up my sattin doublet and cloth hose and cloke lined with plusche and som tobaccoe, and put the other tobaccoe in the binn. Pray send up my swyte.

Sir John was to prove a good friend to Charles I, during his own imprisonment. Cecil Aspinall-Oglander's *Nunwell Symphony* (1945) is a factual counterpoint to Evelyn Waugh's *Brideshead Revisited,* tapping into the same post-war nostalgia for landed gentry, their history and their grand houses – the minutiae of their everyday lives. *Nunwell Symphony* is the biography of one such house, Nunwell. Oglander looks back over almost a thousand years in the life of a family who came over from France with William the Conqueror in 1066. It is both ironic and all too typical that the house passed out of their ownership in 1980 at the start of what was to be a decade of 'selling off the family silver'.

Nunwell uses family letters and documents to bring history to life, through its effect on one family, a kind of aristocratic Archers. The interest lies in the detail, as in the account of the archery craze of the early 19th century. *Lady Holmes gave a very smart Archery Fete at Westover. There were 170 people there, and two prizes, worked by Miss Holmes – a papercase for the gentlemen and a sort of worked arrow for the ladies.* The book ends with the Nunwell Home Guard assembled, then stood down – shades of *Dad's Army* – beneath ancient trees which had heard the Armada's cannon in 1588 watching the still larger Armada of D-Day. *The forgotten gardens droop their neglected heads in sorrowful disarray.* But Nunwell still stands serene, with the same welcoming smile.

To reach **Bembridge** return along **New Road** towards Sandown and at **Marshcombe Shute,** turn left and follow the road through to the village. In the first part of his autobiography, *The Moon's a Balloon,* Bembridge serves as a refuge for British film star, David Niven. He always returns to Rose Cottage (whereabouts unknown) on breaks from boarding school. He also makes his first serious money.

> *Brian Franks and I formed the Bembridge Sailing Dinghy Club for children between twelve and eighteen. At the end of the first season, this club showed a profit of £2.12.6d which Brian and I transformed into liqueur brandy. We were both found next morning, face down in some nettles.*

Niven was a man of many parts, and published a novel *Round the Rugged Rocks* (1951) which is now extremely rare. His two volumes of autobiography were beautifully rewritten, even if Sheridan Morley's *The Other Side of the Moon* (1985), shows how Niven actually rewrote many events of his life for dramatic effect. But Morley confirms that *Bembridge was where his love of sailing really started, and he never lost it.*

The diarist Francis Kilvert visited Bembridge in July 1875, having walked over from Sandown. He captured the sense of time suspended that the village still evokes.

> *The morning was blue and lovely with a fresh breeze blowing from the sea. Bosomed amongst green, pretty cottages peeped through the thick foliage and here and there a garden shone brilliant with flowers. A long beautiful road, dark, green and cool and completely overarched with trees, led towards the sea and in a high meadow the haymakers in*

*their white shirt sleeves, the dark horses and the high loaded waggon
stood out clear against the brilliant blue waters of the channel.
At the edge of the avenue the bright blue sea was framed in a perfect
round low arch of dark foliage. A woman sat solitary under the trees
looking across the sea and the only sounds that broke the peaceful
stillness were the rustling of the firs and poplars overhead and the
clapping of the white sail of a pilot boat as it flapped idly from the yard in
the soft sea breeze.*

Abraham Elder – a kind of precursor of Alfred Hitchcock – in *Tales of the Isle of Wight*
(1843) tells of a fisherman called 'Old Anthony' who smuggled brandy from France. He
went missing on one such trip and his wife walked the shore looking for a sail. One night,
by moonlight, she saw what appeared to be his boat and ran to greet him. The agony lies
in the precise detail Elder employs . . .

*He looked well and hale, though rather thin, and wore his
broad-brimmed hat cocked a little on one side, just as usual. She ran
down to meet him, and clasped him, as she thought, in her arms. But to
her horror, instead of finding his dear old body pressing against hers,
she felt as if she had leaned against a dry stick. She looked up, and saw
that the object she had embraced was nothing but a rough pole , with a
lobster pot stuck on the top of it. It was only one of the booms that were
fixed in the edge of the sand to point out the channel into the harbour.
She looked about in vain for her dear Anthony, and then she looked for
the boat, but that had also disappeared; and old Anthony and his boat,
with the tan sail with a white patch in it, were never seen or heard of
more.*

Clive Egleton, the thriller writer, lives in Bembridge, as does Cliff Michelmore, who
attended Bembridge school. Michelle Magorian, whose *Goodnight Mr Tom* was awarded
both the Library Association's Carnegie Medal and the Guardian Award for children's
fiction in 1982 also lives here. Author of over half-a-dozen books for children, Michelle
performed in her own one-woman show, *The Pact,* at Quay Arts in Newport in 1998.

Another resident, Tessa Krayling, previously worked for the BBC, and as a teacher.
She has written over twenty books for children including *A Dinosaur Called Minerva* and
How To Write For Children. She has lectured widely and teaches creative writing.

Seaview is an exclusive seaside village reached from Bembridge by way of **St Helens**
and **Nettlestone.** It is home to a number of professional writers including Elizabeth
Daish, author of the bestselling *Coppins Bridge* saga and – under other pseudonyms – a
considerable number of medical romances, and Joyce Windsor author of *A Mislaid
Magic* and *A Fierce Unicorn,* published in 1994 and 1996 respectively. Born in Kent,
Joyce lived in Liverpool, Putney in South London and Dorset before retiring to the Island
in 1982 following the death of her husband.

David Hughes is renowned both as an experimental novelist – his ten published
works include *The Pork Butcher* and *But For Bunter* – and a writer of non-fiction,
including a study of J B Priestley and *Seven Ages of England.* In *The Little Book* (1996),
he combined the two forms in an extraordinary fashion.

Hughes was in his early sixties when in 1991 he was diagnosed to be suffering from
cancer of the kidney. Following major surgery, he recuperates at a relative's holiday

home in Seaview. *I faced a good sweep of the Solent through long windows, a heap of pillows at my back.* The summer is as idyllic as one would expect to someone who has recently cheated death, and now relishes every living moment. Hughes plans a perfect book, one he has no intention of writing. The very process of planning it is part of his recovery to rude good health.

Ryde is about three miles from Seaview by way of **Pondwell Hill** and **Appley Road.** Henry Fielding (1707-1754) was stranded here for ten days in 1754, the year of his death. His ship anchored off the town awaiting a favourable wind. *Our ladies went ashore and drank their afternoon tea at an alehouse there with great satisfaction. Here they were regaled with fresh cream to which they had been strangers since they left the Downs.*

Fielding and his wife lodged in an apartment he presumed to be *an ancient temple, built with the materials of a wreck, and probably dedicated to Neptune.* He greatly enjoyed Ryde, whose gravel soil was . . .

> *always so dry that immediately after the most violent rain, a fine lady may walk without wetting her silken shoes. As to its situation it is, I think, the most pleasant spot in the whole island. I confess myself so entirely fond of a sea prospect, that I think nothing in the land can equal it; and if it be set off with shipping, I desire to borrow no ornament from the terra firma. A fleet of ships is the noblest object which the art of man hath ever produced; and far beyond the power of those architects who deal in brick, in stone, or in marble.*

On re-embarking, Fielding had himself seen his face as containing *marks of a most diseased state, if not of death itself.* The ghastliness of his appearance frightened women and earned jests and insults from the sailors and watermen. He had to be hoisted aboard in a chair, and died later that year.

For William Wordsworth (1770-1850), Ryde represented a haven from the revolutionary turmoil of Paris. He looked over from St Thomas's Church towards Spithead and observed the preparations for war.

> *I beheld the vessels lie,*
> *A brood of gallant creatures on the deep;*
> *I saw them in their rest, a sojourner*
> *Through the whole month of calm and glassy days*
> *In that delightful Island which protects*
> *Their place of convocation – there I heard,*
> *Each evening, pacing by the still sea-shore,*
> *A monitory sound that never failed, The sunset canon.*

W Wordsworth: The Prelude Book X (1805/1850)

Wordsworth's brother John was a sailor, who loved the Island. He drowned in 1805 when his ship foundered in Weymouth Bay. William's elegy remembered happier days;

> *And full of hope, day followed day*
> *While that stout ship at anchor lay*
> *Beside the shores of Wight*

William Wordsworth: To the Daisy

Another shipwreck, that of the Titanic, was relived through the memories of survivor Edith Haisman by Ryde author, James Pellow. Edith lived long enough to see her story *A Lifetime on theTitanic* published in 1995.

> *"I'll see you in New York", Edith's father called out as the lifeboat began its journey down into the water. With that, he and the Reverend Carter relinquished their places at the deck-rail, and stepped back into the ever-increasing crowd. The pungent smell of the cigar her father was smoking, and his last words were to stay with Edith for the next eighty or more years.*

Edith Haisman signs copies of her book – *A Lifetime on the Titanic* – at **Ottakars** bookshop in **Newport** on the Isle of Wight in 1995 with Ryde author James Pellow in attendance.

Those who queued for Edith Haisman's signature on publication day in Ottakar's Bookshop, Newport, myself included, felt an odd frisson at being so close to the little, white-haired old lady, crouched in her wheelchair whose feet had actually trodden the Titanic's decks on that fateful voyage so long ago. Here was history fast becoming legend and Edith's death a year or so later has made that process even more imminent.

In 1987, like the Kraken surfacing from the depths, the French submersible, Nautile, brought to the surface a black leather Gladstone bag containing a pocket-watch belonging to Edith's father, drowned on that fateful night. A photograph of the watch – corroded by eighty years immersion on the sea-bed – appears on the back cover of James Pellow's book.

Karl Marx came to Ryde with his wife in 1874 and stayed in **Nelson Street.** He had been forbidden by his doctor to read, but nonetheless *studied all the rather numerous*

109

The biographer of the Beatles, the Rolling Stones, Elton John and Buddy Holly – Philip Norman - knew **Ryde Pier** well. His father ran the amusement arcade there.

Karl Marx came to **Ryde** with his wife in 1874 and stayed in **Nelson Street.** One doubts he did any serious writing though.

Island newspapers available at that time as well as his landlord's books. One doubts he did any serious writing though.

The poet Pennethorne Hughes was born in Ryde in 1907. He wrote *The Isle of Wight: A Shell Guide* and *Thirty Eight Poems* (1970) selected by Geoffrey Grigson, with recollections by John Betjeman and John Arlott, two of the many poets and broadcasters he had helped and encouraged.

The novelist Olivia Manning (1908-1980) author of the *Balkan* and *Levant* trilogies (filmed for television as *Fortunes of War)* died in Ryde Hospital. Her ashes were scattered in the grounds of Billingham Manor.

Anyone who has ever enjoyed a foaming pint of real ale is directed to Ryde resident Kevin Mitchell's *Ryde Pubs – An Illustrated History* (1996) a true labour of love. Here, in a single volume are chronicled the stories of the 'Hand in Hand', the 'King Ludd', the 'Falls of Niagara', the 'King Arthur' and dozens more repositories of legend and malted hops. Never can the sheer, often unseen grind of research that any decent book requires have been so pleasant!

Peter Norris claims to have derived similar enjoyment from compiling his 1997 book *Footlights and Silver Screen.* Subtitled *An Illustrated History of the Theatres and Cinemas of the Isle of Wight,* Norris's book tells the stories of over fifty such places of entertainment, many of which have long since disappeared.

Raymond Allan, author of *Some Mothers Do Have 'Em* was born on the Island, worked as a reporter on the local paper and did ten years of washing dishes and cleaning at a Ryde cinema while attempting to become a professional writer. His first real break came with writing one-liners for TV variety shows. After years of that, fame descended almost overnight from his creation of accident prone, half-daft Frank Spencer, played so convincingly by Michael Crawford. Like Rowan Atkinson's Mr Bean – no great difference really – the near wordless comedy crossed language barriers and became a hit all over the world. Ray once told me that Frank was based largely upon himself, though a Ryde library assistant of the time is also a strong candidate. Ray Allan has also written two stage plays, and continues to hope that lightning will strike twice.

Anthea Cohen lives in **Dover Street,** and was once a sister at the former Royal Isle of Wight County Hospital in Ryde. She now writes novels in which a hospital sister kills people she dislikes (and is never found out!). *Angel in Autumn* (1995) is the first with an Island setting although Anthea has so far written thirteen books in the *Sister Carmichael* series as well as a number of novels for teenagers.

Philip Norman – the biographer of the Beatles, the Rolling Stones, Elton John and Buddy Holly – grew up literally on **Ryde Pier.** His father ran the amusement arcade, and his experiences fuel one of the finest autobiographical novels written since the Second World War. *The Skaters' Waltz* (1979) is an extremely detailed account of life in Ryde in the 1950s, an urban *Cider With Rosie.*

The novel opens in **Trinity Street.** A ground floor flat in Holmwood, a fading Ryde mansion is the childhood home of the young hero, Louis. Across the road is Holy Trinity Church, *a church so big that it was practically invisible, only its spire betrayed it,* and through whose graveyard Louis walks to school. A left turn and a short walk downhill and you would be in **Monkton Street.** Louis's father has left home, but without warning he returns, *as if they had met yesterday.* The novel then goes into flashback. It is 1947, and the four-year old Louis has just moved to the Island with his parents, yet the longer he

Philip Norman's autobiographical novel The Skater's Waltz opens in **Trinity Street, Ryde.** Across the road is Holy Trinity Church, *a church so big that it was practically invisible, only its spire betrayed it.*

lives there, *the deeper grew his impression of a temporary home, a life misrouted and in abeyance.*

Norman is like an English Proust in his recall of childhood wonder, pin-sharp descriptions of the town. *Towards the bottom, Union Street abandoned its regal descent and lapsed into a nearly perpendicular gradient to which the last shops clung like climbers on a rock face.* His parents take over a casino and rifle range on the pier. A fisherman shows Louis a hermit crab, *frightening, like red fingers groping from a shell,* while his father expands his army of slot machines, and opens a roller skating rink, in a desperate attempt to remain financially afloat. The novel's great tension lies in the simmering relationship between his parents, which the young boy barely understands, and it ends with an unsuccessful attempt by his father to leave, with young Louis in tow.

> *As we come to the end of the pier – as the railway curves to its terminus, and the Pavilion is revealed on its stilts down the long estuary – I feel myself, at long last, beginning to cry.*

The promised sequel has never appeared, apparently because Norman found it too painful to revisit his adolescence. However, *Everyone's Gone to the Moon* (1995) is a novel based on his career as a colour supplement journalist in the 1960s. That swinging decade is depicted as evocatively as is the 50s in *A Skater's Waltz,* as also is the *Sunday Times* in its great heyday and, some might say, the young Tina Brown on her way to superstardom. The hero is now called Louis Brennan, which strongly suggests that this is the second novel in a series. One can only hope that Norman one day fills the gaps between and after: here is potentially a sequence of novels to rival Balzac in their razor sharp accuracy and lack of nostalgia.

The Age of Parody: Dispatches from the Eighties (1990) does the same for the decade of greed, though in short reprinted articles rather than fiction. Here is the whole of Britain – rather than just Wight – as Fantasy Island. Norman has also published *Words of Love* (1989), a collection of tender short stories, *Wild Thing* (1972), a concept album of narratives from the world of rock music, and *The Road Goes on Forever: Portraits of a Journey Through Contemporary Music* (1982).

There is an interesting interview in *Isle of Wight Rock* (1994), which reveals that his father's pier complex had been called the Seagull Ballroom – where rock bands played in the late 60s. His father painted the Seagull's grand piano grey, with yellow keys. When he replaced it with a Hammond organ, he simply heaved the piano into the sea.

> *And it floated, just floated away. They watched it for hours, you know sort of making its way out to Spithead.*

As Norman said later, *I have travelled the world, interviewed Colonel Gadhafi, but I have never encountered people like I met in Ryde in the 50s.* He also remembered going into the Mayfair Café, run by the Minghella family, hearing *'Let's Go to the Hop',* and seeing *this little boy running around.*

The *'little boy'* was Anthony Minghella, celebrated film director and writer of the feature films *Truly, Madly, Deeply* and the multiple Oscar-winning *The English Patient* as well as a huge volume of television material from *Grange Hill* and *On The Line* to *Inspector Morse.*

Never one to shy away from the big themes, life, love, death, Minghella shares Fellini's lightness of touch, where sadness and pathos can break out into sudden humour or domestic tragedy. *Mr Wonderful* is a film set in a seaside resort in winter, *it was like a version of my life growing up on the Isle of Wight;* he was born in Ryde and educated at Sandown Grammar School. He went on to Hull University to study drama: his play about Richard II *Two Planks and a Passion* (1984) was directed by Danny Boyle at Greenwich, while Michael Codron produced *Made in Bangkok* (1986), an exposé of the British abroad.

Minghella then moved into ground breaking work for television – notably the trilogy *What If It's Raining,* and radio, the Giles Cooper Award-winning *Cigarettes and Chocolate* (1989). He has also written extensively for children, as in Jim Henson's *The Storyteller.* Like Bob Dylan, Minghella has never looked back.

Or rather he did, in an unexpectedly moving Radio 4 documentary. Broadcast in 1997, *The Fool Who Goes Or The Fool Who Goes Away* (a quote from Samuel Beckett), Minghella talked to the Abbot of Quarr Abbey, where he once went on retreat, to friends who had pursued careers in music, and his father, still making ice cream from a factory in Wootton. Anthony's younger brother Dominic has followed him into the TV business, writing scripts for *Hamish Macbeth.*

Ryde has produced a fair number of literary eccentrics. Stephen Adam, a songwriter and composer of *The Holy City,* was once Mayor. He was also the brother of James Maybrick, a leading contender for the real Jack the Ripper, according to *The Diary of Jack the Ripper,* edited by Shirley Harrison.

Alan and Hilary Hadcroft have written *Seven Times a Prisoner* (1993), an eerie tale based on fact about seven sisters housebound in East Upton, near Ryde, and an autobiographical account of another kind of entrapment, *DHSS The True Story* (1995).

Maurice Bronson now lives in Ryde. He appeared on TV as the would-be headmaster of *Grange Hill* and as Adolf Hitler in *Indiana Jones and the Last Crusade* and wrote entertainingly of his adventures in *Yes Mr Bronson – Memoirs of a Bum Actor* (1997).

David Icke moved to Ryde while still a sports commentator for the BBC: he had been forced to retire early as a professional goalkeeper due to arthritis. Icke wrote his early books here before going on to declare himself a Son of God. He co-founded Island Watch, which helped save Ryde Pavilion and other threatened buildings, and became prominent in the Green Party. His polemic *It Doesn't Have To Be Like This* still reads as a convincing indictment of a throwaway society, and some conspiracy theorists – myself included – wonder if an unnatural influence had been brought to bear since his more recent books by implication largely discredit what has gone before. *The Truth Vibrations* and *The Light of Experience* (1993) are either works of fantasy or profound truths, only time will tell. Icke certainly taps into that rich vein of the elemental Isle of Wight, which has attracted everyone from the monks of Lyra to the followers of Gurdjieff, and from Keats to Gascoyne, but he cuts it with bathos.

> *The Isle of Wight felt like home because in past lives it had been, and my electro-magnetic programme was designed to be attracted and drawn by the energy field of the Island . . . we had our honeymoon at the Claverton Holiday Flats on the sea front of Ryde.*

Leaving Ryde for Newport by way of **Binstead Road** and **Quarr Hill,** Quarr Abbey is on the right. The original abbey with its tide mill was founded in 1132, but the quarry predated it, and supplied its stones. The Cistercian order was dissolved in 1536 along with other monastic communities by Henry VIII. A later spate of religious persecution saw the Benedictine monks of Solesmes in France escape first to Appuldurcombe and then to Quarr. They built the current monastery in 1908, from a design by one of their number, Dom Paul Bellot in coloured Belgian brick.

Robert Graves was an early visitor, moving from Osborne to the newly opened guest house, used as a convalescent home for soldiers recovering from action in the First World War. In *Goodbye To All That* (1929), he looked back to the mess and misery of the fighting from which he had been invalided out with acute bronchitis.

> *Hearing the fathers at their plain-song made me for the moment forget the war completely. Many of them were ex-Army officers who had turned to religion after the ardours of campaign or disappointments in love. The Guest Master showed me a library of twenty thousand volumes. There were all kinds; history, botany, music, architecture, engineering, almost every other lay subject. I asked whether they had a poetry section. He smiled kindly and said, no, poetry could not be regarded as improving.*

Graves admits to half-envying the Fathers their abbey on the hill.

> *Those clean whitewashed cells and meals eaten in silence at the long oaken tables, while a novice read 'The Lives of the Saints'! The food, mostly cereals, vegetables and fruit, was the best I had tasted in years – I had eaten enough ration beef, ration jam, ration bread and cheese to last me a lifetime. At Quarr, Catholicism ceased to repel me.*

Woodside Bay reached via **New Road** in **Wootton,** was the site of the second Isle of Wight Pop Festival, held over August Bank Holiday weekend, 1969. Philip Norman came back to his native Island to report the event for the *Sunday Times*. In *Shout* (1981), his definitive history of the Beatles, he wrote that . . .

> *If you were young, you headed south to the Isle of Wight, to green chalk downs where Keats and Tennyson once walked, and where half a million now pitched their tents to hear a poet comparable in stature, though barely believable as a presence under any such small-time seaside sky. Dylan had agreed to appear, emerging from long seclusion in America to play on the grassy slopes above a British holiday camp.*

Fernhill today is a small turning off **Station Road** in Wootton, but in the late 18th century, it was the name of the home of Thomas Orde, Governor of the Island at that time. A turreted house, now demolished, it stood at the head of Wootton Creek, and commanded fine views of the Solent. *The grounds rank amongst the finest in the Island. The shrubbery extending to Wootton-bridge, and the plantations throughout, are flourishing and luxuriant. The arbutus abounds here in perfection.* The house itself, though, was *not quite calculated to convey a favourable idea of the erector's taste,* surely an insult too far!

It was here that the sixty-three year old composer Joseph Haydn came to stay in July 1794, and played in the drawing room which he reckoned *commands the most magnificent view over the ocean.* The distinguished composer was taken to see Orde's other residence on the Island – Carisbrooke Castle – and Newport, which he thought a *nice little town.*

Station Road, left at the top of the **High Street,** leads ultimately to **Havenstreet,** home of the Island's remaining steam railway stock. Tennyson talked of ringing down the endless grooves of time, thinking that this was how trains moved. There is a flourishing railway literature about the history of steam locomotion on the Island, with books such as Andrew Britton's four-volume set, *Once Upon a Line* (1983 onwards) chockful of the personal reminiscences of those who actually worked the main line. Havenstreet, where the station and a single track to Wootton in one direction and Smallbrook in the other have been miraculously preserved along with some locomotives and rolling stock looks like the setting for an episode of *The Avengers.*

In 1878, Henry James was less convinced by the magic of steam.

> *The Isle of Wight is at first disappointing. I wondered why it should be, and then I found the reason to be the influence of the detestable little railway. There can be no doubt that a railway in the Isle of Wight is a gross impertinence, is an evident contravention to the natural style of the place. The place is pure picture or it is nothing at all. It is ornamental only – it exists for exclamation and the water-colour brush. It is separated by nature from the dense railway system of the less diminutive island, and is the corner of the world where a good carriage road is most in keeping. Never was a clearer opportunity for sacrificing to prettiness; never was a better chance for not making a railway.*

Colin Pomeroy compiled *Isle of Wight Railways: Then And Now* (1991), an act of creative industrial archeology which returns us to an era as remote now as that of the dinosaurs. At Blackwater, for example,

> *renamed Brambles, the station house has been enlarged to provide a family home, the extension being built over the ground previously occupied by part of the platform; not the merging of the old and new roof tiles. The greenhouse stands in front of where the shelter and toilets once were. How many casual observers, though, would connect this rural spot with the railways of the first half of the 20th Century.*

My personal favourite is in **Betty Haunt Lane** near Carisbrooke, where the road abruptly rears up and over a bridge which appears to surmount nothing but a field.

The Age of Steam is at its zenith in the *'Lestrade'* detective novels by M J Trow, who lives in Havenstreet, and teaches history at Ryde County High School. Trow has published sixteen Lestrade books so far, and like guiltily purloined sweets, I devour each one as it comes into the bookshops. The premise is both simple and endless. The Scotland Yard detective so patronised in Conan Doyle's original Sherlock Holmes canon is here made rounded flesh and blood, a put-upon but painstaking professional who always gets his man, while Holmes is a vain poseur, in need of Sholto Lestrade's help.

Each plot gives Trow the opportunity to wrest a puzzle from an historical setting, whether it be the Titanic, Peter the Painter, prize-fighting or the Victorian music hall. The glory or curse of these books lies in Trow's sense of humour, juvenile or hilarious according to taste.

> *"Excuse me", he said in his truculent Cockney, "are you two policemen by any chance?"*
> *Dickens looked at his feet. Was it that? Or his helmet-shaped head that had betrayed him?*

To my mind, this kind of thing serves as both distraction and antidote to the fiendish cunning in the plots of these novels, and the flashes of genuine hurt and emotion that reside in the title character.

Trow is now working with a new lead, Peter Maxwell, a widowed teacher. *Maxwell's House* is the first in the series, with a planned TV tie-in. He has also written a fine non-fiction exposé of the Bentley and Craig murder case in *Let Him Have It, Chris* (1990) and *The Many Faces of Jack the Ripper* (1997). This latter book provides *a complete account of the gruesome crimes that appalled Victorian society, and contains the first full lineup of suspects, (more than thirty people are listed) including FBI profiling techniques and in-depth psychological analysis.*

Chapter Six – Cowes, Newport & Carisbrooke

Osborne House in East Cowes belongs to English Heritage and attracts several hundred thousand visitors each year. Queen Victoria loved the place and wrote, after it had been purchased for her in 1844 *it is impossible to imagine a prettier spot; we have a charming beach quite to ourselves – we can walk anywhere without being mobbed.*

Prince Albert rebuilt Osborne largely to his own design, with the help of Thomas Cubitt, the first (and poshest) volume builder. Using the latest construction techniques, with a cast iron frame, Albert created a dream palace, an Italian villa with a first floor balcony and towers, set over a view that he compared to the Bay of Naples. It is no coincidence that Victoria's drawing master was Edward Lear, famed for his delicate watercolours of Italian landscape as much as for his nonsense verse.

Tennyson dedicated his *Idylls of the King* to Albert, the model of a perfect gentleman, and made frequent visits to Osborne from Farringford. After Albert's early death – in 1861 – Victoria largely retreated to Osborne, from where she ran her Empire.

The poet Jeremy Hooker has captured today's stuffed feel of Osborne and its treasures, the sense of being suffocated by history.

> *Among her many possessions*
> *The Empress of grief*
> *Becomes her statue,*
> > *marble*
> *Among marble and horn,*
> *Silver and ivory, mahogany and teak*

Jeremy Hooker: At Osborne House

For many years the official *Illustrated Guide to Osborne* contained a 'Catalogue of Furniture, Pictures and Works of Art' compiled by one Anthony F Blunt Esq, Surveyor of the King's – and then the Queen's – Pictures. His predecessor was Sir Kenneth Clark, whom history has treated with greater sympathy.

Queen Victoria's correspondence with the Poet Laureate has been collected in *Dear and Honoured Lady* (1969) and edited by Hope Dyson and Charles Tennyson. In a letter dated July 1885 – signed, for the first time, 'yours affectionately' – the Queen even suggests that Tennyson persuade Gladstone, then Prime Minister, that he should retire from politics . . . *radicals wish to push him on at 75½ to do what will ruin his reputation more than this last government has already done.* As Tennyson would willingly have consigned Gladstone, his old rival for Arthur Hallam's affections, to a bath of serpents, this must have been gratefully received.

Arnold Florance's *Queen Victoria at Osborne* (1977) – a book dedicated to 'Charley my parrot and constant companion' – gives a sanitised account of Victoria's friendship with John Brown, though it does quote her letter saying *I must find consolation where I can.* Osborne was recently used as one of the settings for a feature film – *Mrs Brown* – based on the friendship starring Billy Connolly as the faithful ghillie, and Judi Dench as Victoria . . . *The quiet countryfolk of East Cowes thought his manner of speaking to his sovereign as 'wumman', telling her to hold her head up while he fastened her scarf, and giving her advice as to her clothes, as impudent beyond bounds.* Florance recalls meeting several locals whose grandparents had felt a strong dislike towards this worthy Scotsman. She closes her book with the curious matter of the royal undergarments, which Victoria had ordered to be burnt after her death, but which seem to have circulated around the Island, as Royal souvenirs. Still, better than a china mug, I suppose.

John Matson's *Dear Osborne* (1978) takes the history of the house beyond Victoria's time, and onto its use as a naval college and a convalescent home for officers, among which was Matson himself. He quotes a letter from Victoria to the Princess Royal, dated July 1858.

> *Osborne is really too lovely – the deep blue sea, myriads of brilliant flowers – the perfume of orange blossom, magnolias, honeysuckle – roses etc. of all descriptions on the terrace, the quiet and retirement all make it a perfect paradise – which I always deeply grieve to leave.*

The Edward VII Convalescent Home housed officers recuperating from the horrors of the Great War. A A Milne spent part of 1917 here in deep gloom, only relieved by his making friends with Robert Graves. They had bedrooms which had once been the night nurseries of Queen Victoria's children, and took *favourite walks through the woods and along the quiet seashore.* Milne wrote,

The Edward VII Convalescent Home at **Osborne** housed officers recuperating from the horrors of the Great War. A A Milne spent part of 1917 here with Robert Graves.

> I know nothing which gives me so complete a feeling of luxurious rest
> as settling down to a novel in a deck chair immediately after breakfast,
> with the knowledge that one is safe from the reproaches of conscience.

In *Goodbye to all That* (1929), Graves recalls the same kind of charmed escape:

> This was the strawberry season and fine weather; we patients could
> play billiards in the royal billiard room, drink the Prince Consort's
> favourite Rhine wines among his Winterhalters, play golf-croquet and
> visit Cowes when in need of adventure. Many of the patients were
> neurasthenic and should have been in a special hospital. A A Milne was
> there as a subaltern in the Royal Warwickshire Regiment, and in his
> least humorous vein.

To bring succour to such sad cases, Graves helped found a Royal Albert Society, *its pretended aim being to revive interest in the life and times of the Prince Consort.* At Osborne one could hardly escape his daily presence. Queen Victoria had kept a place for him in her bed for years after his early death. Graves notes,

> My regalia as president consisted of a Scottish dirk, hessian boots and
> a pair of side-whiskers. Official business could not proceed until the
> announcement had been made that 'The whiskers are on the table'.

To join, one had to have some connection, however tenuous, to Albert. One must profess oneself a student of his life and work, or come from Alberta in Canada, hold the Albert medal, work in the Albert Docks etc. One successful applicant was the grandson of the man who had built the Albert Memorial. But drunken behaviour soon gave these imposters away as officers come to break up the society, agents provocateurs.

> They began giving indecent accounts of the Prince Consort's private
> life, alleging that they could substantiate them with photographic
> evidence. I got worried, it was not that sort of society. As President, I
> rose and told in an improved version the story which had won the 1914
> All-England Inter-Regimental Competition at Aldershot for the filthiest
> story of the year. I linked it up with the Prince Consort by saying that he
> had heard it from the lips of John Brown, in whose pawky humour
> Queen Victoria used to find such delight; and that having prevented him
> from sleeping for three days and nights, it had been a contributory
> cause of his premature death. The interrupters threw up their hands in
> shocked surrender.

Among other nonsensical games was one of changing all the labels in the Osborne Art Gallery. *Anything to make people laugh. But we found the going hard.*

The architect John Nash (1752-1835) built East Cowes Castle as his own residence. The man responsible for the design of Regent's Park and Regent Street in London and rebuilding the Royal Pavilion in Brighton, also designed the Guildhall in Newport on the Island (but not the dreadful tower which was added later). He also designed the Isle of Wight Institute, Northwood Church and St James in East Cowes, where he now lies buried, as well as remodelling Northwood House and Nunwell. East Cowes author, Ian Sherfield, has written extensively about Nash in *East Cowes Castle* (1994).

He reproduces random entries from Nash's diary: on Christmas Day 1832, *James Pennethorne and Mr J M W Turner came – went to Whippingham Church – stayed the Sacrament.* The steam crossing over to West Cowes was rough, which doubtless Turner enjoyed more than most. On an earlier visit in 1827, Turner gave three paintings to Nash – 'Cowes Regatta', 'Sailing in the River, and 'The Music Room of the Castle' – all now in the Tate Gallery.

Later in his life, financial problems forced Nash to return to East Cowes for good, and to live in near poverty, such was the thanks of a grateful nation. His final job of work was the construction of St James Park in London. By 1835, he was in fading health.

> *Monday May 4th. Took a little castor oil in the morning – sat up in the evening to have the bed made and be shaved.*
> *Tuesday May 5th. Not able to get out of bed without assistance. Sleeping all day, Mrs Nash ill.*
> *Wednesday May 6th. Very ill indeed all day.*
> *Sunday May 10th. Very ill.*
> *Monday May 11th. Much worse.*

Nash died two days later. The inscription on his tomb did not even record his profession, and the *Annual Register* merely stated that *as a speculative builder this gentleman amassed a large fortune, but as an architect he did not achieve anything that will confer upon him a lasting reputation.* His friend the satirical writer Theodore Hook (1788-1841), successful editor of the Tory *John Bull* (the *Private Eye* of its day), and a prolific and popular novelist showed more generosity and more foresight.

> *Look at the manner in which St James Park was in a few months converted from a swampy meadow into a luxurious garden, and then let the reader ask himself whether the metropolis is or is not indebted to the taste and genius of the most traduced object of this notice. In private life, Mr Nash was a warm and sincere friend, his mind active and comprehensive as it was, was singularly natural and simple; his thoughts were original, and his conversation was both instructive and pre-eminently agreeable.*

East Cowes Castle was wilfully demolished early in the 20th century, and the town itself heavily developed by industry and housing, among which distinguished old houses of the Osborne Estate stand out, like diamonds in the rough. *Discovering East Cowes* (1994), compiled by East Cowes Heritage is a good walking guide to the area.

Use **Cowes Floating Bridge** (it has a book all to itself, *Discovering the Floating Bridge at Cowes* (1995) by Sarah Burdett) to cross the Medina to **Cowes.** Thomas Arnold (1795-1842), headmaster (1828-1842) of Rugby public school, and father of Matthew Arnold (1822-1888), the poet, was born in Cowes. His family lived here for two generations: he looked back to a happy childhood – *I was brought up in the Isle of Wight, amidst the bustle of soldiers, and from childhood familiar with boats, ships and flags of half Europe.* Arnold and his family lived at 'Slatwoods' and the boat store arches can still be seen built into a newer house.

Neville Shute who once lived and worked in Cowes, gave three of his novels Island settings. *What Happened to the Corbetts* (1939) prefigures the air raids which were shortly to devastate the area, and is set around the Solent, Wootton Creek, Newtown and

The prestigious Royal Yacht Squadron is located in what was once **Cowes Castle**. In 1650 it served as a prison for Sir William D'Avenant, unofficial poet laureate to the recently executed Charles I, and a friend – some say the illegitimate son – of William Shakespeare.

Yarmouth. *Requiem for a Wren* (1955) deals with a later stage of the War, that leading to D-Day and involves the friendship between a young Wren and two Australian servicemen. *Stephen Morris* (1961) is about the pioneer days of aviation at Bembridge, sailing in the Solent, Cowes, the Needles and the Nab Tower.

The prestigious Royal Yacht Squadron is located in what was once Cowes Castle. It is easily found off **The Parade** in Cowes. Sir William D'Avenant (1606-1668) was imprisoned here in 1650. Unofficial poet laureate to the recently executed Charles I and a friend – some say the illegitimate son – of William Shakespeare, D'Avenant had been knighted in 1643 at the siege of Gloucester during the Civil War. A fierce Royalist, he had left France for Virginia on Queen Henrietta Maria's behalf, but was captured by a Parliamentary ship, and brought to prison on the Island. Here he began writing *Gondibert,* a poem of chivalry which, when he was taken to the Tower of London for execution, he said *was interrupted by so great an experiment as dying.* It is said that Milton interceded on his behalf and he was released on bail in 1652. He was a fine poet:

> The lark now leaves his wat'ry nest,
> And climbing shakes his dewey wings.
> He takes this window for the East,
> And to implore your light he sings.

In 1915, The Castle was turned into what Robert Graves described as *the most exclusive club in the world,* where he would drink gin and ginger, while *sweeping the Solent with a powerful telescope.* Its distinguished history is told in Montague Guest and William

123

Boulton's *Memorials of the Royal Yacht Squadron* (1903). A somewhat breezier account of both club and sport is to be found in Anthony Heckstall-Smith's *Sacred Cowes* (1965) while Occomore Sibbick's *Lulworth Shared My Playground* (1996) is a superb history of the cutter Lulworth, and of Cowes itself during the great regattas of the 1920s. The author lives in East Cowes.

Heckstall-Smith writes . . .

> *In those halcyon days, Cowes regatta was the culminating function of the Season. The aristocracy of England, who had, in theory, enjoyed one another's company since the previous May, went off to their grouse moors in Scotland, and to their country estates. The visiting Crown Heads – and there were still many of them – sailed away in their great steam yachts. It was all rather silly, snobbish and utterly artificial. Half those who graced the Squadron lawn did not know port from starboard or a cutter from a schooner. They were there to see and be seen or because to be there had become a habit. For most of them, the ambitious mamas, the eager daughters and the ardent young men, Cowes was yachting and yachting was Cowes.*

A tougher, more professional breed of sailor provided all-year-round entertainment. Uffa Fox was a brilliant raconteur, a shanty singer, a yacht designer, a friend of everyone from the Royals to pub low-life. In his local, the Buddle Inn – he owned a large house in Niton – he held a weekly cabinet meeting, pretending to be Prime Minister, and putting the nation to rights. It is with Cowes, however, that Uffa Fox will forever be associated, and his spirit lives on in a series of racy autobiographies and sailing manuals. Books like *Handling Sailing Boats According to Uffa* (1960), and *Joys of Life* (1966), capture wit and wisdom in equal parts.

> *Remember, too, that like fire the sea is a good friend but a bad master; so you must never, never allow yourself to get into the position where the sea takes control.*

Techniques are explained in a rough and ready way which has in some cases been overtaken by the politically correct.

> *In these days of nylon spinnakers you have to keep something on your forestay; because if the damp spinnaker wraps around wire it grips as tight as the clothes on those women you see who fill them so well that you think they have been poured into them, and somebody forgot to say "when".*

Another venerable old Cowes resident was Captain 'Trader' Horn. *Way For A Sailor* (1979) is dedicated to his *beloved and neglected 'Gollywog'* but, that solecism aside, here is a watery Island childhood par excellence. No wonder the locals proudly call themselves 'caulkheads', because they float!

> *We would 'borrow' a boat from the waterfront and tide her the four miles up the river on the flooding tide, window-shop in what seemed to our minds a huge metropolis, and back to Cowes on the fast-running ebb. I still think this no mean feat of seamanship. Our sole propellant was the tide, using the bottom boards as sweeps for steering. If the wind was*

fair we flew the weirdest jury rig imaginable. With a length of driftwood lashed to a thwart as a mast, we ran free with sails made up of shirts, coats and even trousers laced together.

In the time of Sir John Oglander, writing in the early 17th century, *there was not above three or four houses,* although the place was already associated with sailing and boatbuilding.

John Keats wrote that

one of the pleasantest things I have seen recently was at Cowes. The Regent was anchored opposite – a beautiful vessel – and all the Yatchs (sic) *and boats on the coast, were passing and repassing it; and circuiting it and tacking about it in every direction – I never beheld anything so silent, light and graceful.*

St Mary's Church is in **Terminus Road.** John Nash was responsible for its elegant tower. Charles and Mary Lamb, joint authors of *Tales from Shakespear* (1807), spent a summer holiday in Cowes in 1803.

We do everything that is idle, such a reading books from the circulating library, sauntering, hunting little crabs among the rocks, reading churchyard poetry, which is as bad at Cowes as any churchyard in the Kingdom can produce.

Westbourne House is in **Birmingham Road,** opposite the Police Station. William Arnold moved here when appointed collector of Taxes in the Isle of Wight in 1777, the year after the colonies in America had declared independence. His son, Thomas – born here in 1795 – was Principal of Rugby School between 1828 and 1842, and his grandson, Matthew, the poet, author of *Dover Beach* (1867). D Arnold-Forster, *At War With the Smugglers* (1936), takes in the whole of William's career, from his training in the Post Office to his early death. Much of the information derives from a newly discovered cache of previously unseen letters. The book has a sharp immediacy as a result.

Cliff Michelmore, writer and broadcaster was born in Cowes in 1919, as Arthur Clifford Michelmore. His father had come to the Island seeking relief from TB, but unfortunately did not survive long. In *Two Way Story* (1986) co-written with his wife Jean Metcalfe, whom he met on air introducing 'Family Favourites', he recalls how *our three up, three down terraced house, three rows back from the banks of the River Medina was crowded when we were all at home.* Cliff was the youngest of six. In an article written for *Hampshire* magazine, he wrote

I was within sight, smell and sound of the gasworks, the River Medina, Whites shipyard, many boatyards, a fish and chip shop, the railway that ran along from Cowes to Newport and carried the almost toy trains that are now denied Islanders. As Autumn came, there was little to remind me of the summer past. Admittedly the photographs in Beken's windows, the delicate tarry smell from the long, low shed of Bannisters Ropewalk and the chemist's shop which displayed in its front windows five-headed dogs and two-headed foxes, the shops with their "By Appoinment" signs would never let us forget where we were, nor what next Cowes Week would bring.

Westbourne House in **Birmingham Road, Cowes,** was the home of William Arnold, Tax Collector for the Isle of Wight who moved here in 1777. His son, Thomas – born here in 1795 - was Principal of Rugby School between 1828 and 1842.

He would play in Shamblers Copse, full of *secret places, where our gang built hides and we played Tarzan,* before moving in with his sister in Baskett's Farm, his first taste of the true country. At the age of sixteen he enlisted with the Royal Air Force, and from there went on to present live television, notably the current affairs programmes *Tonight* and *24 Hours,* before presenting BBC Television's *Holiday* for over eighteen years.

The American poet, Ezra Pound visited the Island while a young man. Although not resident here for any length of time, he later wrote *My European Inception has begun . . . with the well donkey at Carisbrooke Castle, Isle of Wight and very large strawberries served with 'Devonshire Cream' at Cowes.*

Gay Baldwin, that avid chronicler of all things ghostly, lives in Cowes. Her books on Island hauntings have sold over a quarter of a million copies world-wide, and benefit from her training as a journalist on the Isle of Wight County Press. *Ghosts of the Isle of Wight* (1977), and its sequels work so well because of their painstakingly researched local detail. In Cowes alone we have ghost on crutches in Newport Road, a curly headed man of about eighteen composed of solid smoke, a Second World War soldier in tin helmet and army greatcoat, a phantom coachman and a Tudor remnant who walks through a wall in a local restaurant.

It was probably at Cowes that the novelist Laurence Sterne (1713-1768), author of the multi-volumed *Tristram Shandy* (1759) – a post-modern epic centuries ahead of its time – stayed with his mother while his father was engaged on military action.

The French poet Paul Claudel saw the Island as rising from the waves, like Venus. *Our first port of call, Cowes, is the most select, the most elegant.* Edward Thomas

126

quotes an earlier poet, whom history has fortuitously rendered anonymous, writing in 1781 the following verse – not so much deathless as dead.

> *See ruddy health with naked bosom stand,*
> *On yonder cliff, and wave a vigorous hand,*
> *Above the banks with florid cheeks that glow,*
> *Pointing triumphant at the tide below;*
> *The pregnant tide with healing power replete,*
> *Where health, where vigour, and where pleasure meet.*
> *Here ocean's breath comes mingled with the breeze,*
> *And drives far off the bloated fiend, disease.*
> *No more to foreign baths shall Britain roam,*
> *But plunge at Cowes, and fine rich health at home.*

Aubrey de Selincourt reckoned, more reasonably, that *nobody who knows Cowes could fail to love it, in spite of the fact that the greater part of the town is even uglier than Ryde.* He could also not resist noticing that the shops in Cowes waste little money on appearance.

I can't help chuckling with pleasure when I see the dilapidated door and modest frontage of a certain sailmakers – "the most famous in the world" – who would make mainsails at three thousand pounds apiece.

Exit Cowes by way of **Queens Road** and **Egypt Esplanade** towards **Gurnard.** The poet Sean Street spent summer holidays here as a child in one of the small wooden palaces which front the Solent, and wrote a poem in 1984, looking back.

> *The thirty years that grew me up*
> *did not happen here.*
> *The small boy standing on the shore*
> *must always have been there,*
> *Watching his toy yacht sail from just beyond*
> *to a sea he will meet again somewhere*
>
> *He walks back to his shanty-house*
> *crying for the lost boat, passing my stare,*
> *but he does not see me – my little ghost –*
> *and the ebb sucks the green beach bare*

Sean Street: The Toy Yacht (1984)

Sean Street now lives in Bournemouth, where he teaches media studies at the University, and is well known both as a broadcaster and a writer. Solent tides also wash through his moving and memorable poetry collection *A Walk in Winter,* a series of elegies for his parents.

Leave the Esplanade by **Woodvale** and **Baring Roads** and follow the signs for **Newport. Oxford Street** is on the right just beyond the traffic lights where **Nodes Road** and **Newport Road** meet. The poet David Gascoyne lives in Oxford Street. Born in Harrow in 1916 and educated at Salisbury Cathedral School and the Regent Street Polytechnic in London, he moved to Paris where he became an important member of the surrealist movement. In 1935 he published *A Short History of Surrealism* and helped organise the first major exhibition of the form in London.

In his introduction for *Facets of an Island,* Gascoyne wrote of his first experience of the Island, *a brief spell as a ship's cook spent on an H M Examination Service vessel patrolling the Solent at the outset of the last War.* He particularly remembered,

> *the congeniality of Yarmouth pubs, and the efficiency of a young woman barber in Newport. I am ashamed to admit that the Island's beauty did not strike me at that time, nor did I even make an effort to visit Farringford, despite a love of Tennyson's poetry that has never left me.*

It was at this time that Gascoyne was writing material later collected into *Poems 1937 – 1942* (1943), illustrated by Graham Sutherland, in which his earlier verbal fireworks deepened into profound art. Living so self-consciously a life of the intellect and pure imagination, left its scars. His recently published *Paris Journal* records despair, near starvation, drug addiction and a lover who later died in a German concentration camp, lit with occasional passages of delight and insight.

In the 1960s, Gascoyne was forced by illness to return to the Island to live with his parents. It was a return he approached with dread:

> *the idea of Island life that I brought with me was epitomised in a dream image that arose in my mind about then, in which drab suburban villas appeared to be filled with sleepy inertia and boredom as though with a poisonous gas. It was not until the writer Edward Upward arrived one day with his car, in which he took me for my very first real tour of some of the Island's most attractive spots, that my eyes began to open to a scenic environment clearly released to the part of the mainland, Hampshire, Wiltshire and Dorset, that I had known so well and deeply loved when a child.*

Gascoyne was later admitted as an in-patient at Whitecroft Hospital near Newport. From these inauspicious surroundings he wrote and published his extraordinary prose work *The Sun At Midnight* (1970) a series of aphorisms on alchemy, visions and drug addiction. *I proclaim the sacred unity of Poetry (spiritual naming and making of essences), and Science. The destructive schism of Two Cultures now no longer need exist.* The book ends with a poem 'in progress', visionary work so far outside the intellectual mainstream as to be an act of bravery:

> *Our gentle sister Memory*
> *Our brother Brute Desire,*
> *Conspire from time to time in Time*
> *To set the World afire.*

This from a poet for whom *my ability to write had completely deserted me, a slough of despond resulting in sterility and lost self-confidence.* Judy Gascoyne (then Lewis), who used to visit Whitecroft to read poetry to the patients, in one of the great love affairs of the century, used the sheer force of her will to drag David from his hospital bed and damaging introspection. She married him in the process, got him back into writing, and even reading his work in public.

Gascoyne's eminence has been hard won, and fellow poets have increasingly beaten a path to the door of his modest, suburban semi-detached house. Tributes, too, the French Government created him a Chevalier for his services to poetry and visitors have included Sean Street – who recorded a programme for BBC Radio 3 – Iain Sinclair, and thriller writer Chris Pettit – who filmed an interview with Gascoyne for a poetry celebration at the Royal Albert Hall. Sinclair later wrote a superb poem about the visit, including an unforgettable image of Gasoyne ascending to his bedroom on his chair-lift like Apollo rising to Heaven.

Other disciples to visit have included Adrian Henri and Jeremy Reed, who like Gascoyne has given his all to literature, at the risk of losing his sanity. Also in attendance have been publishers Alan Clodd and Stephen Stuart-Smith of Enitharmon (who retained faith in Gascoyne when the major presses had allowed his work to go out of print) the novelist Amanda Hemingway and – most moving of all – Aidan Dun, whose work Gascoyne himself credits with energising him again as a poet. I was privileged to witness their first meeting, and as electricity seemed to literally crackle in the air, was aware of a flame being very consciously passed. At his 80th birthday party, poet Anthony Rudolf talked movingly of Gascoyne's encouragement and grace to a secular congregation of fellow writers, family and friends. Gascoyne had recently barely survived a serious fall, and the prediction enshrined in *November in Devon* written in 1986 seemed ominously close.

> *At half my age this might have worried me more.*
> *The South country kept my childhood secure.*
> *Now I know that to Whinny-moor*
> *Before long I shall come, as one more year*
> *Declines towards departure in deceptive calm*

In fact, David made a good recovery and began writing poems again, one of which – about ivy seen through his bedroom window – was published by the *Independent* newspaper on his birthday in 1996.

Gascoyne has been energised by reading the work of Aidan Dun and Iain Sinclair, and has talked recently about writing an Island variant on *Lud Heat,* a psycho-geographical survey of the locality. This would tie in with his desire that . . .

> *I would wish to write one or two landscape poems about those neglected or seldom frequented areas of the Island where I have occasionally been reminded that despite the inevitable ravages of commercialism and ecological pollution, "for all this", to quote Gerard Manley Hopkins, "nature is never spent; there lives the dearest freshness deep down things". And it is my idea of the Island as a place both in and out of time that causes me fervently to concur with those other words of Hopkins:*
>
> *"O let them be left, wildness and wet*
> *Long live the weeds and the wilderness yet".*

Some of Gascoyne's early work appears in *Seeds in the Wind – 20th Century Juvenilia* (1989), edited by Neville Braybrooke. Braybrooke lives for part of the year in Northwood and is currently researching material for a biography of G K Chesterton, to whom he is related.

Gascoyne ends his introduction to *Facets of an Island* by quoting a prose poem – available before only in a privately printed, limited edition pamphlet – by Humphrey

Jennings, the documentary film-maker and founder of Mass Observation, who was involved with Gascoyne in the early days of the surrealist movement.

A Picture in the Victoria and Albert Museum is inspired by a painting by Victorian artist Richard Burchett of a view looking towards Whitecliff Bay near Bembridge. It is high Summer and the harvest has just been gathered in. A woman dressed in blue walks towards the observer; another sits by the path, with white chalk cliffs looming behind her.

> *What minutiae of music in the blue of the breathless channel, in the dazzlingly white fossil fish, in the depths of the yellow corn, on the cheeks of the woman under the blue parasol, in the heart of the woman under the shadow of noon*

Continuing towards Newport, on the left almost opposite the entrance to St Mary's Hospital in **Parkhurst Road,** is Albany Prison. Named after the Duke of York and Albany and built in 1798, during the French Revolution, John Keats complained to his friend John Hamilton Reynolds in April 1817 that

> *I saw some extensive barracks which disgusted me extremely with Government for placing such a Nest of Debauchery in so beautiful a place – I asked a man on the coach about this – and he said the people had been spoiled. In the room where I slept at Newport I found this on the window "O Isle spoilt by the Milatory!" I must in honesty confess that I did not feel very sorry at the idea of the Women being a little profligate.*

The prison opened in 1963, on the site of these barracks, to house some of the most dangerous men in Britain. Contemporary folk demons – stars of their own cult literature – like Moors Murderer Ian Brady, the Yorkshire Ripper and the Kray twins have spent time here. Indeed the late Ronnie Kray was a published poet in his own right, and a very good one, I hasten to add. Among his favourite themes was his love for his mother and the delightful nature of kittens.

In *Inside the Firm* (1991), Tony Lambrianou – a henchman of the Kray Twins – is affronted that *there were reports that Mafia-style rackets involving gambling and villainy were being operated at Albany, and that Chris* (his brother) *was behind them. I had never been to Albany prison, so I decided to sue the five newspapers that named me. Chris's part in the Albany disturbances came to an end with the beating up he was given by the screws, and his transfer, injured, to* (next door) *Parkhurst.*

Church Litten is a green space roughly in the centre of **Newport.** In one corner stands the Lord Louis Library. In fact, the first librarian of the Bodleian Library in Oxford, Dr Thomas James was born in Newport in 1570. Just seven years before him, the poet Richard Eades (1563-1631), chaplain to Elizabeth I, was born *ye sonne of a clothier who dwelt at ye corner house in ye beastmarket in Newport.* Eades amazingly anticipated Shakespeare by writing a tragedy entitled *Julius Caesar* in 1582, some fifteen years earlier than the Master.

A headstone enbedded in the wall around the library bears the legend *The Friend of Keats.* It commemorates the death of John Hamilton Reynolds who died in 1852 – possibly by his own hand – and who is buried here.

J H Reynolds began his working life as an insurance clerk, who also wrote poetry. His father was the writing master at Christ's Hospital. In 1814, at the age of eighteen, he published *Safie, An Eastern Tale,* an oriental novel that appeared to owe much to Byron.

John Hamilton Reynolds, whose headstone in **Church Litten** proclaims *The Friend of Keats,* took rooms at 36 Nodehill, Newport which he converted into offices of the County Court. Unfortunately he died a drunkard and a gambler.

He became an early friend of John Keats and they corresponded regularly. Reynolds inspired Keats to write *Isabella, Or the Pot of Basil* (1818) which he intended to supplement with some of his own verse in a volume of Boccaccio, although he only contributed two tales towards the project. These were published in *The Garden of Florence in 1821.*

Keats found Reynolds to be the *playfullest of the three witty people in the set,* despite being dubbed by highbrow critics as the 'Cockney' school. During his stay in Carisbrooke, Keats summoned Reynolds over from the mainland to join him – in vain – as well as dedicating one of his first mature poems 'To J H Reynolds Esq.'

Dear Reynolds! I have a mysterious tale,
And cannot speak it: the first page I read
Upon a lamplit rock of green sea-weed
Among the breakers; 'twas a quiet eve,
The rocks were silent, the wide sea did weave
An untumultuous fringe of silver foam
Along the flat brown sand.

In turn, Reynolds wrote in 1820 to the *Edinburgh Review* on Keats' behalf, *his health is now in the worst state, for as his medical man tells me he is in a decided consumption, of which malady his mother and brother died. By his friends he is very much beloved, and I know of no one with such talents so unaffected and sincere.*

Ironically, Reynolds did end up on the Isle of Wight, some years after Keats death. He worked as assistant clerk of the County Court at Newport. As Edward Thomas wrote,

> the literary promise of his youth had not been belied, but had remained simply unfulfilled. He took to the law and married, and for some reason that was an end of him. This gives a fortuitous touch of pathos to his early serious and humorous verses, so full of life, if not of genius itself. He wrote a poem at the age of seventeen which Byron praised. He parodied Wordsworth's 'Peter Bell'. Under the name of Peter Corcoran he wrote a lovable little book called 'The Fancy' in which he celebrated and dismissed his youth with much humour.

That book was reprinted with illustrations by Jack B Yeats and with an introduction by John Masefield, who wrote *he loved poetry, but he loved life and nature more.* As to Reynold's decline, in the words of Lord Ernle,

> he was promoted to County Clerk when he took a seven-year lease from John Poore on number 36 Nodehill at £35 a year, occupying rooms which he converted into offices of the County Court. He professed himself to be an Unitarian and a bitter Radical, and whose drunken habits placed him beyond the pale of society.

He died a drunkard and a gambler. *The law spoilt his literature, and his love of literature and society interfered with the drudging duties of the lawyer.* The romantic poet gone hopelessly wrong.

Charlotte Mary Mew (1869-1928) was born in Bloomsbury, daughter of a well-to-do London architect. Her great grandfather was Benjamin Mew, the brewer, and an uncle kept the Bugle Inn in the High Street. The family spent every summer at Theirn Farm in Newfairlee just outside Newport. Penelope Fitzgerald told of their arrival in *Charlotte Mew and Her Friends* (1984),

> At Newport they were met by their aunt from the farm, with a wagonette for the luggage and a fly for the children. On one occasion, the tiny impetuous Lotti (Charlotte) jumped up to take the seat by the driver. When Elizabeth Goodman checked her by rapping her sharply over the knuckles with a parasol, Lotti is said to have seized the parasol and snapped it in half. She was intoxicated by the open air, the fields of

standing corn, the estuary with ships made fast at the quay and the chequered lights and shadows of the Newport Downs.

The young Charlotte wanted to go *homewish* in the Island dialect, which she was discouraged from using. She wrote it into an early poem about an Island beach at night, phosphorescent with a strange light:

Heer's the same little fishes that splutter and swim,
Wi' the moon's old glim on the grey, wet sand;
An' him no more to me nor me to him
Than the wind goin' over my hand.

On Sunday evenings, the family would walk to the new church at Barton (St Paul's in Staplers Road, Newport) through fields edged with dog-roses, *a short life when I could pray, years back in magical childhood.* Sunday was, for the young poet, *a day of eyes.* She soon lost her religious faith, but not that sense of Eden.

The holiday would culminate with a visit to Newport market, for *Bargain Zadderday.* This was a hiring fair straight out of the pages of Thomas Hardy, but for the young Mew it became an image of terror, its denizens *grinning end to end.* Charlotte homed in on the terror and strangeness which so often lies beneath the Island's beauty, storing up images that would haunt her for the rest of her life: a coffin carried out of a silent house, a ship sinking quietly with the loss of all hands, and – again soundless – a dead rat in the road.

Notice how the appearance of this horrible object is made even more dreadful by the way the line is uncapitalised and indented, starting further into the page like someone catching their breath.

I remember one evening of a long past Spring,
Turning in at a gate, getting out of a cart, and finding
*   a large dead rat in the mud of the drive.*
I remember thinking: alive or dead, a rat was a godforsaken thing,
But at least, in May, that even a rat should be alive.

This image – the stiff body, the fine hair inside its ears – haunts her final short story, unfinished because beset by increasing family and financial difficulties that curtailed her literary activities, she committed suicide.

Indeed another poem, about a girl concealing under her shawl either a pregnancy or an aborted child, *the red, dead thing,* is set back in the Newport market of her childhood.

In the white of the moon
On the flags does it stir again? Well, and no wonder!
Best make and end of it; bury it soon.

Saturday Market

The irony is that no-one can care less: in *Saturday market nobody cares.* Here is the embryonic confessional school of Sylvia Plath and Anne Sexton. Mew has likewise become a feminist icon. The American female writer, P B Parris, has produced an extraordinary tour-de-force in *His Arms Are Full of Broken Things* (1994), an imaginary autobiography as if written by Mew herself, and heavily dependent upon Fitzgerald's trail-blazing biography

I cherished sunshine memories of the freedom I'd found on the island, charging down the steamer's gangplank and clambering up onto the open carriage at the landing with seagulls bickering overhead, hide-and-seeking in haycocks on Uncle Richard's Newfairlee farm, shouting and shooting the flock of maddened chickens, climbing trees – impossible, unthinkable in London – windfalls in the apple orchard, pigeons and dog roses, cider and gingerbread, noisy piglets and a silent dead rat in the lane.

In a house in the **High Street,** Elizabeth Sewell, daughter of a Newport solicitor, wrote her many stories for girls. Mary Gleed Tuttiett, who wrote under the pseudonym Maxwell Gray, was the daughter of a Newport doctor. Two of her best known poems refer to the loss of domestic pets – not a dead rat in sight. She is best remembered for her novel *The Silence of Dean Maitland.*

Another Newport resident, Albert Midlane, wrote the hymn *There's a Friend for Little Children Here,* while John Dore produced *Vectis Lays* (1878) and versified local legends, which after Mew's work is like weak beer as a chaser for neat arsenic.

The roads to Carisbrooke Castle are well signposted. **Castle Road** is on the left where **The Mall** becomes **Carisbrooke Road.** Canterbury House is about halfway up on the left. John Keats stayed here in April 1817 as a guest of Mrs Cook. His room directly overlooked the Castle, a view now obscured by buildings and trees. On arriving, he wrote a letter to his friend J H Reynolds, complaining that he had not yet written a single word of a long poem he had in mind. And yet inspiration was about to strike.

I intend to walk over the Island East-West-North-South. I have not seen many specimens of ruins – I don't think however that I shall ever see one to surpass Carisbrooke Castle. I see Carisbrooke Castle from my window, and have found several delightful wood-alleys, and copses, and quick freshes. As for Primroses – the Island ought to be called Primrose Island: that is if the nation of Cowslips agree thereto, of which there are diverse clans just beginning to lift up their heads.

It was in the grounds of the Castle that Keats began his first major poem, *Endymion* (1818).

A thing of beauty is a joy for ever:
Its lovliness increases; it will never
Pass into nothingness; but still will keep
A bower quiet for us, and a sleep
Full of sweet dreams, and a health, and quiet breathing.
Therefore, on every morrow, are we wreathing
A flowery band to bind us to the earth

The most notable inhabitant of Carisbrooke Castle is probably Charles I. In 1647 he was captured by Fairfax's New Model Army and held at Hampton Court Palace. On November 11th, he escaped to Titchfield and thence to Cowes, where he spent the night at the Plume of Feathers. He then rode on to Carisbrooke in the hope that the newly appointed Governor, Colonel Robert Hammond, a cousin by marriage to Oliver Cromwell, would afford him protection. At first he was a guest – albeit one with guards at

John Keats lodged at **Canterbury House** in **Castle Road, Carisbrooke** as a guest of Mrs Cook in April 1817. His room directly overlooked the castle, a view now obscured by building

his door – but after the defeat at Preston in August 1648 of the invading Scottish army and thus the end of hopes to restore him to the throne, he became a closely guarded prisoner.

The Earl of Clarendon, in *History and Documents* (1647), records how *notwithstanding the strictness with which the king was guarded, many persons found means to present themselves to him at his usual times of walking within the lines, in order to be touched for the disease called the king's evil.* Magic still attached itself to anointed royalty. It was while imprisoned in the Castle that the King wrote his poem *Majesty in Misery.*

> *But for refusal they devour my thrones,*
> *Distress my children and destroy my bones.*
> *I fear they'll force me to make bread of stones*

Charles also composed the self-justifying prose work *Icon Basilica.* As Winston Churchill was later to write, *here, where a donkey treads an endless waterwheel, he dwelt for almost a year, defenceless, sacrosanct, a spiritual King, a coveted tool, an intriguing parcel, an ultimate sacrifice.*

The Romantic poet John Sterling, fired with revolution, took a different view before locking himself away in Bonchurch forever.

> *That death has held his carnival*
> *While armies mustered round its wall,*
> *And that through many a month's long round*
> *A despot here his dungeon found.*

Carisbrooke Castle

A letter survives, dated May 1648, written to Edward Worsley of Gatcombe – Z – by Charles himself – J – and concerning a Colonel Titus, W. It involves the King's second attempt to escape, but its cipher would hardly tax John Le Carré.

> *Z: I finde so good fruits in the paines that you take for me that againe I must put you to a little more trouble (asseuring you that you shall finde me thankfull to you for altogether, & that, not in a meane way) it is, that you would goe to Southampton, to one Mrs Pits howse, where you will finde W: & deliver to him the enclosed . . . I would not have any bodie know that I have written to him: So I rest. Your most asseured frend. J.*

Such strategems proved useless: Charles was moved by the Army to the chillier confines of Hurst Castle in December 1648, and within two months had lost his head. As the Anti-Pragmaticus had predicted a year before, *he forsook paradice for this Isle, and when he leaves it and comes to his Palace at Westminster, it's but a step to heaven.*

Much has been written about Charles' involuntary stay on the Island. The best factual account by far is *The Royal Prisoner* (1965) by Dr Jack Jones, for many years Curator of the Castle Museum, and now the Island's most respected historian. His successor, Roy Brinton, has written a number of books on different aspects of the Island's history. The Castle Museum houses Tennyson's writing desk from Farringford, and the poet's hat and coat.

Jack Jones reprints letters from the King to Mary, the assistant laundress, a historical fact which Margaret Campbell Barnes turned into fiction in *Mary of Carisbrooke* (1956), a graphic account.

Carisbrooke Castle whose most notable inhabitant was Charles I in 1647. From here he wrote his poem *Majesty in Misery.*

*The laundry casements stood open to let out the steam, and at a
wooden tub stood Mary, her work-a-day brown dress bunched up over
a gay quilted petticoat, washing the King's body linen.*

This might not be great literature, but it certainly remains a good read. The dialogue and
descriptive passages of *Mary of Carisbrooke* are as fresh as the day it was written, or as
Mary Floyd's newly washed laundry. There is a liveliness here missing from so much
historical fiction. The book is one of a series of novels by Barnes, many written or
completed at her homes in Wellow, Yarmouth and Freshwater on the Island. Among
them are *The Passionate Brood* (1954), *Within the Hollow Crown* (1948, revised 1958),
Brief Gaudy Hour (1948), *With All My Heart* (1951), *The Tudor Rose* (1953), *Isabel the
Fair* (1957), *King's Fool* (1959), and *The King's Bed* (1961).

Subsequent visitors to Carisbrooke Castle have generally been awestruck by such an
historic setting. All, that is, except Dorothy Osborne (1627-1695), who once lived in
St Lawrence where she met William Temple (1628-1699) in 1648. In her *Letters,* written
to him during the period 1652-54, and which were finally published in 1888, she tells how
she and her brother scratched a biblical quotation on a window. Summoned before the
Governor, she confessed and was released. The young William Wordsworth was taken
around by an ancient guide who proudly informed the poet that he had cradled the dying
General Wolfe in his arms at the Battle for the City of Quebec in 1759.

Swainston Manor, now a hotel, was once the home of Sir John Simeon, a good friend of Alfred Lord
Tennyson. The original building was the summer palace of the Bishops of Winchester. Edward I stayed
here in 1285 and Edward II visited in 1320. Ownership later passed to Richard Neville, better known as
Warwick the Kingmaker.

John Keats visiting in 1817, found that time had healed old wounds . . .

the Trench is overgrown with the smoothest turf, and the walls with ivy.
A colony of Jackdaws have been there for many years. I dare say I have
seen many a descendant of some old cawer who peeped throught the
bars at Charles the First when he was there in Confinement.

Leave Newport by way of **Carisbrooke High Street** and **Calbourne Road.** Swainston Manor is located on the right after approximately three miles. This was once the home of Tennyson's friend, Sir John Simeon. It was Sir John who made the original suggestion that the poet create *Maud* out of a few stray lines of verse. Tennyson was later to sit under a *dark cedar . . . sighing for Lebanon* on the day of Sir John's funeral, and write the following lines . . .

Nightingales warbled without
Within was weeping for thee;
Shadows, of three dead men
Walk'd in the walks with me,
Shadows of three dead man and thou wast one of the three.
Nightingales sang in the woods:
The Master was far away:
Nightingales warbled and sang
Of a passion that lasts but a day;
Still in the house in his coffin the Prince of courtesy lay.

In the Garden of Swainston

There has since been a dispute in the letter columns of the Isle of Wight County Press about whether the original tree was blown down by the Great Storm of 1987.

Emily Tennyson's *Journal* for May 1870 records the family's reaction to Sir John's passing.

The terrible blow of Sir John Simeon's death fell on us just as we were
starting for Aldworth. A. goes to Swainston for the funeral. All dreadfully
sad & trying & seeming all the sadder that the sun shone and the roses
bloomed profusely.

The original building was the summer palace of the Bishops of Winchester, and Edward I stayed here in 1285. Edward II visited in 1320, and ownership later passed to Richard Neville, better known as Warwick the Kingmaker.

It has remained a place of good fellowship. John Oliver Hobbes wrote in 1902, that *I would like to take you to Swainston (Sir Barrington and Lady Simeon's place); Tennyson really wrote Maud there; they are also charming people.*

Dick Francis, the champion jockey turned best-selling crime novelist, pays tribute in a book on the best loved hotels in the world to his stay at Swainston in the summer of 1993. *I can honestly say that we have never stayed in a more comfortable hotel with such a welcoming atmosphere.*

On the hill opposite is a more brooding memorial, an 18th century copy of a Greek temple. Seen briefly through the trees, it can still infuse the imagination with thoughts of depravity and sacrifice.

A cottage opposite All Saints Church in **Calbourne** (the rear of the two shown) was the birthplace of W H Long in 1838, a farmer's son who compiled the *Isle of Wight Dialect Dictionary* in 1886.

Turn left at the crossroads in **Calbourne** into **Lynch Lane.** A cottage opposite All Saints Church was the birthplace of W H Long (born 1838, year of death uncertain), a farmer's son who compiled the *Isle of Wight Dialect Dictionary* in 1886. He was attempting to capture a dying tradition, and the book contains songs, jokes and anecdotes to embroider the definitions. Here is the definition of *Pitchen Prong,* a pitchfork.

> *I spooas ye don't mind Jan White, the fiddler, what used to live at Moortown in Brison parish: – but there, he was dead avore a you was born. He was as miserable rum sort o' feller, and a used to zing in church one time. In the fall o' the year, one evenen, I was gwyne by his house, and 'twas raainen pitchen prongs we' the vorks downwards; and there zet Jan on top o' the pig's hourse, in his shirt sleeves. "Hullo, Jan!" zays I, "whatever bist up to there?" "Well, mayet", a zays, "I be tryen to ketch a good coold, zo I shall be aable to zing base in church next Zunday".*

The punctuation is as eccentric as the dialect and there is oral folk poetry in what, at first, sounds like gibberish. But rain can be exactly like falling pitchforks if it is heavy enough, and there is a certain mad logic in the fiddler's reply.

One of the Rectors of Calbourne was Nicholas Udall (1504-1556), the author of *Ralph Roister Doister* (1553), commonly reckoned to be the first English comedy.

The long drive that leads to Westover House begins on the left at the entrance to the picturesque, much photographed, **Winkle Street.** Octavius, a younger brother of Elizabeth Barrett Browning (1806-1861) lived here, and the Moulton-Barretts (whose original wealth came from plantations in Jamaica), continued to occupy Westover until early in the 20th century. Local gossip has it that Robert Browning visited Octavius, and from him heard the legend of the Pied Piper of Newtown. Using poetic license, he relocated the story to Hamelin in Germany.

Elm Lane begins on the other side of the crossroads and joins the **Yarmouth Road** at **Shalfleet.** Our journey of discovery is almost over with only one place remaining – **Cranmore,** a mile or so from Yarmouth. Travel writer John Coleman lives here. *Coleman's Drive* (1962) tells of his determination to drive a vintage Austin Seven through the deserts and jungles of South America, and then the length of North America to New York. It is a car mechanic's nightmare.

> *It soon became clear that the trouble lay inside the magneto. I removed the cover and to my horror saw inside only a mass of brass and fibre fillings. I was miles out in the desert and the piece of mechanism that produced that vital spark had minced itself into a thousand minute particles. I sat down on the road, and kicked my heels into the dust in silent despair.*

Those familiar with Island roads will know the feeling!

As we approach **Yarmouth,** the road from Cranmore suddenly opens up to give a magnificent prospect of the Solent – due north. To the south are salt marshes, flooded in winter, neatly bisected by the embankment that once carried the steam railway. The road is a relatively new affair: a Victorian mansion, the Mount, was demolished to accommodate it.

Ron Winter's *The Ancient Town of Yarmouth* (1981), a definitive history of the town, ends by quoting a homily uttered by the Mayor on the occasion of Elizabeth II's Silver Jubilee. *Make us the joy of the present, and the praise of ages to come.* Words of farewell.

Porters summoning passengers for the departing ferry used to cry out *This Way for England.* Charles Tennyson Turner, brother of the Poet Laureate, captured this same sense of a forced return to the everyday.

> *Silent I gazed upon our foaming wake,*
> *And silent on the Island hills I gazed,*
> *As up the ebbing stream we bore,*
> *to make Our harbour, while the West athwart us blazed.*

In her short story *The Red-haired Miss Daintreys,* Rosamond Lehmann writes about the ferry ride back to Lymington.

> *Now comes the best of the voyage, when the boat leaves the channel and begins to wind through the ribbony deep-fretted flats to the pier and the harbour. Far over the expanses of glowing burnt sienna mud, a growth of luminous and tawny rice grass is blocked in as if with a palette knife. The same sea-gulls perch top-heavy upon the white stakes that mark the estuary's course; other waterfowl skim and scuttle across the marshes. Small sailing craft float past us, running before the wind on a wing of red, white or tan sail. They wave to us, we wave back. Receding, they stay fixed, an illustration, between blue water and blue sky. Till next summer, next summer.*

Alfred Tennyson wrote *Crossing the Bar* on his last ferry journey back to the Island, in October 1889. As he travelled over from Lymington, he jotted the words down on an envelope, while waves broke over the sandbar between Hurst Castle and Totland. Back in his study at Farringford, he wrote them out by candlelight and read them to his nurse *"will this do for you, old woman . . . "*. Hallam Tennyson was moved to tears.

> *"That is the crown of your life's work". He answered, "It came in a moment". He explained the 'Pilot' as "that Divine and Unseen Who is always guiding us". A few days before my father's death he said to me: "Mind you put 'Crossing The Bar' at the end of all editions of my poems".*
>
> Hallam Tennyson: Tennyson, A Memoir (1897)

First though, my own poetic answer, half parody, half tribute.

> *The voyage back was ceremonial*
> *that ship stately as a lost queen,*
> *a cigarette and a beer at the bar,*
> *my car waiting locked and forlorn -*
> *The voyage back was ceremonial.*
>
> *The difficulties of saying farewell –*
> *A country where once I was King,*
> *The dying gleam of an evening star,*
> *Bleak sunlight on the opposing shore –*
> *The difficulties of saying farewell.*
>
> Brian Hinton: The Voyage Back

And now for two stanzas of the real thing.

> *Twilight and evening bell,*
> *And after that, the dark,*
> *And may there be no sadness of farewell,*
> *When I embark.*
>
> *For tho' from out our bourne of Time and Place*
> *The flood may bear me far,*
> *I hope to see my Pilot face to face*
> *When I have crost the bar.*

It is the great magic of the written word, that it endures and continues, that it can be accessed at any time or place, just by opening a book or switching on a computer. I hope that this journey upon paper will have encouraged the reader to track to their source some of the brief and, of necessity, severely edited passages I have glanced at as we travelled. To investigate further the lives of the writers we have discovered, in a bookshop or a library.

> *This is always happening; the discovery, or re-discovery of a bit of real writing. Jack Horner work – you put in a thumb. For example, this morning I wanted a book, any book, and my hand fell on Tennyson's 'Idylls of the King'. I read*
> > *. . . He was a mute:*
> > *So dark a forethought roll'd about his brain,*
> > *As on a dull day in an Ocean cave*
> > *The blind wave feeling around his sea-hall*
> > *In silence . . .*
>
> *And I stared in delight, my mind possessed by the evocative image of the "blind wave". Living as I do not far from Tennyson's old home, I know every story about the vain old monster, but immediately they were cancelled out, forgotten, and the seedy Victorian lion becomes a magician, another Merlin, and I salute him in gratitude, admiration and wonder. For if any man thinks it is easy to write like that – let him sit down and try it.*

J B Priestley: Delight (1949)

Postscript

Julian Barnes is one of the best known novelists in Britain, with *Metroland, Flaubert's Parrot* and *A History of the World in 10½ Chapters,* as well as non-fiction detours like *Letters from London,* a brilliant survey of the dog days of the Thatcherite revolution. *England, England* (1998), is his first novel for six years, *a book about England, about the **idea** of England – and about the search for authenticity and truth amid the fabulation and bogusness that is "England".*

Where better to set such a study than the Isle of Wight – and so he does. Like Auden before him *"this island now"* serves as a metaphor for a nation, troubled and unsure of its future, trapped in the afterglow of Empire. The blurb begins with a cliché, which Barnes has turned into a modern legend. *"As every schoolboy knows, you can fit the whole of England on the Isle of Wight".* The grotesque, visionary tycoon Sir Jack Pitman takes the saying literally. He constructs on the Island 'the Project', a vast heritage centre containing everything 'English' from Buckingham Palace to Stonehenge, from Manchester United to the White Cliffs of Dover.

Just the kind of thing, in fact, to receive a large grant from the Heritage Lottery Fund, and an obvious parody of New Labour's plans for the Millennium Dome at Greenwich. *The project is monstrous, risky and vastly successful. Indeed, it gradually begins to rival 'Old England', then to supersede it, then to offer itself as a sort of model society of the future.*

This is the kind of vision which makes even Golden Hill's game plan – a millennial Pop Festival, screened around the world, and an 'edutainment' centre based on information technology – seem very small scale, indeed. Barnes takes the Island's representational quality, a chalk 'O' which somehow contains the whole world, and turns it into a gigantic theme park. This is not as improbable as it might first seem. Some years ago the Disney organisation laid serious plans to buy up the Island as a massive fun factory. Some of the more extreme conservationists would like to see the place as a managed natural paradise, rather like the dinosaur island in *Jurassic Park.* At the end of *Wight: Biography of an Island* (1985/1997), Paul Hyland calls instead for sympathetic economic development, in tune with the Island's rich history, and with regard for its natural beauty. His final image is that of an oil rig between Wight and Purbeck which *plumbs the depths.*

In **Discovering Island Writers**, I have sampled just a tiny cross section of the multiplicity of moods and narratives with which writers have invested this small piece of land, squeezed between the Solent and the English Channel. The Island is narrow, yet endless and it contains eternity in every grain of sand:—

History draws me homeward, past lowering hedgerows, and the steady sea to my own silence, writing these very words. Each generation we make our imprint on the fresh-laid sand for darkness, like a tide, to cover us up, to render us unheard.

Brian Hinton: Just Desserts (1989)

Index of Writers